VISIONARY LEADERSHIP IN SCHOOLS: SUCCESSFUL STRATEGIES FOR DEVELOPING AND IMPLEMENTING AN EDUCATIONAL VISION

ABOUT THE AUTHOR

Dr. Edward W. Chance is currently an assistant professor in the Department of Educational Leadership and Policy Studies at The University of Oklahoma. He is also the Director of the Center for the Study of Small/Rural Schools. He previously was the Supervisor of the Educational Administration program at South Dakota State University. Dr. Chance has been a classroom teacher, assistant principal and principal in both urban and rural settings. He is a certified Reality Therapist and has utilized that discipline model over the years. He holds a Ph.D. in Secondary Administration from The University of Oklahoma. Research interests include developing viable field experiences for potential administrators, leadership, rural schools, and vision building.

VISIONARY LEADERSHIP IN SCHOOLS:

SUCCESSFUL STRATEGIES FOR DEVELOPING AND IMPLEMENTING AN EDUCATIONAL VISION

By

EDWARD W. CHANCE, PH.D.

CHARLES C THOMAS • PUBLISHER
Springfield • Illinois • U.S.A.

Published and Distributed Throughout the World by

CHARLES C THOMAS • PUBLISHER
2600 South First Street
Springfield, Illinois 62794-9265

© *1992 by* CHARLES C THOMAS • PUBLISHER

ISBN 0-398-05784-2

Library of Congress Catalog Card Number: 91-44478

With THOMAS BOOKS *careful attention is given to all details of manufacturing
and design. It is the Publisher's desire to present books that are satisfactory as to
their physical qualities and artistic possibilities and appropriate for their particular
use.* THOMAS BOOKS *will be true to those laws of quality that assure a good
name and good will.*

Printed in the United States of America
SC-R-3

Library of Congress Cataloging-in-Publication Data

Chance, Edward W.
    Visionary leadership in schools : successful strategies for
developing and implementing an educational vision / by Edward W.
Chance.
        p.   cm.
    Includes bibliographical references and index.
    ISBN 0-398-05784-2
    1. School management and organization—United States.
    2. Leadership.   I. Title.
LB2805.C44   1992
371.2′00973—dc20
                                                                91-44478
                                                                CIP

To Patti

FOREWORD

The terms vision and visionary leadership are new additions to our professional vocabulary. One could make an extensive list of the waves of words adapted and adopted by our profession. Frequently, the words are incorporated into the daily lexicon before clear definitions or applications of the terms are identified.

Educators are ready to rally around the need for vision and visionary leadership in our schools. However, we are in search of someone to point the way. We need a means of identifying vision and a means of assisting individuals who want to develop their visionary leadership skills.

The development of visionary leadership is critical because of the challenges education faces. As educators are asked to respond to issues such as those raised by *America 2000,* restructuring, choice, and financial constraints, a new leadership will be required.

These new leaders will need clearly articulated beliefs, commitment to attaining their goals in schools, ability to create the shared ideology necessary to achieve the goals of the school, risk-taking ability, innovativeness, and a view of the future that is significantly better than the present. These characteristics describe the visionary leader.

Edward Chance provides a framework for developing visionary leadership. By identifying both the theoretical basis as well as specific methods for developing visionary leadership, Chance bridges the theory—practice domains of educational administration.

Chance's treatment of the subject of visionary leadership reflects both his academic credentials as well as his extensive experience working with school districts throughout the United States. His contribution to the literature concerning visionary leadership is timely and significant.

MARILYN L. GRADY, PH.D.
University of Nebraska-Lincoln
Lincoln, Nebraska

vii

CONTENTS

VISIONARY LEADERSHIP IN SCHOOLS: SUCCESSFUL STRATEGIES FOR DEVELOPING AND IMPLEMENTING AN EDUCATIONAL VISION

Chapter I

EDUCATIONAL REFORM
IN THE UNITED STATES

Reform. Restructuring. Redesigning. Career Ladders. Site Based Management. Outcome Based Education. Lead Management. Collegiality. Empowerment. Shared Decision Making. These terms represent only a partial list of the concepts and ideas to bombard the educational system in this country during the past decade. The result of the advocation of such postulates found policy makers and political leaders racing to implement and mandate new curricular guidelines, increased graduation requirements, mandatory testing of students, explicit extensive certification requirements, and expanded, albeit often unrealistic, societal expectations. Add to this picture financial chaos in numerous states and school districts as the result of lawsuits and court decisions condemning inequitable and unequal funding formulas.

It is no wonder that the view of a large portion of the general populace became one that perceived the country's educational system as second rate, outmoded, and decrepit. Too many believed the economic woes experienced were the direct result of a shoddy, antiquated institution. School leaders were often forced into a response mode that was both managerial and reactive. Visionary and proactive leadership became a thing of the past as schools were inundated by state and federal mandates, rules, and regulations. The absence in this country, or in local districts, of an individual and collective vision led to confusion, disenchantment, and an increased organizational disequilibrium.

THE REFORM MOVEMENT

Where did this reform begin? How did it evolve? How has it influenced schools? What impact has it had on schools? This reform movement began ostensibly with the publication of *A Nation at Risk* (1983). This relatively small document which took two and a half years to produce served as the catalyst for this reform cycle. The remarkable thing is that the cycle has lasted so long, although it has evolved through several stages or waves (Murphy, 1990; Sergiovanni & Moore, 1989). Reform is not new to education in this country. Cycles seem to come and go each decade. Some impact the system, many do not.

The Committee of Ten on Secondary School Social Studies in 1893 recommended changes in the educational curriculum that would provide an expanded academic nucleus of English, history, mathematics, science, and foreign language. By the end of World War I, The Cardinal Principles of Secondary Education (1918) signaled another reform effort which advocated a varied curriculum that instigated the rise of the comprehensive high school. The 1930s fostered the concept of progressivism with an expanded, more diverse curriculum. The 1940s saw the publication of the National Education Association's report *Education for All American Youth* (1944) which provided public schools the opportunity to develop life adjustment curricula which further varied the academic offerings.

The 1950s contributed a reform movement that was deeply concerned about the absence of rigor in the curriculum as well as the quality of teaching. As is often the case, politics and political concerns came to the fore in this reform cycle. James Bryant Conant's report on high schools provided education with new math and new science as part of the answer. The political and educational scramble to maintain industrial and technological superiority would persist into the mid-1960s. The late 1960s and early 1970s found a sense of chaos in both school and society as the country attempted to understand and interpret the meaning of Viet Nam. This same period saw a change in the type of youth that schools were called on to educate, as the number of minority and lower income students increased and the cultural diversity of the nation became even more apparent. The late 1970s brought a call for a return to the basics and the re-establishment of a core curriculum.

Obviously educational reform, actual or perceived, is a continuous, cyclical process in this country. Each cycle creates new problems, resurrects old ideas, places blame, and too often seeks easy, simplistic answers concerning complex issues. Each reform cycle begins in a similar manner with various articulated concerns about the quality of education provided by schools. Task forces and study groups are established and given the charge to ascertain solutions to the perceived problems and issues. Task forces traditionally include business and lay citizens, public officials, concerned taxpayers, and occasionally educators. Reform policies, rules, or regulations are advanced that often do little but temporarily satisfy the public and politicians. Cuban (1990) argues that there "are really tactical moves to ease political tensions over the role of schools" (p. 139). After the policies are adopted there generally is a time of relative peace before the reform cycle begins anew. The uniqueness of this reform movement is its longevity and its impact on both public and higher education. The current effort has endured at least two, and possibly three, waves of reform (Bacharach, 1990; Murphy, 1990; Sergiovanni & Moore, 1989).

The first wave of reform was exemplified by reports such as *The Nation at Risk* (1983), *Action for Excellence* (1983), *High School* (1983), *Educating Americans for the 21st Century* (1983), and *A Place Called School* (1984). These and other like-minded reports exhibited certain similarities and commonalities. Sizer (1983) identified seven trends that were evident in the first wave of reform. These were:

1. A call for a return to the basics.
2. A concern about understanding and strengthening the relationship between schools and the economy.
3. An appeal for the resurgence of adult authority over students and the schools of this nation.
4. A belief that the state, not the federal government, should serve as the agent of reform.
5. An assertion that the financial cost of schools and education must be reduced.
6. A conviction that the diverse needs and abilities of students should be met by establishing several different types of schools. It was maintained that the students and their parents should have a degree of choice in selecting an appropriate school.
7. An opinion that students and their schools need to be evaluated as to their performance and that this could best be accomplished by utilizing measurement techniques that seek to ascertain the results of teaching and learning (p. 1).

The first wave of reports resulted in the development of numerous policies which were often implemented at the state level and bureaucratically imposed on local school districts. Although in the past these actions might have settled the reform issue, it did not do so this time. Indeed, policies of this first wave were barely written and disseminated when the criticism began. Much of the criticism and repudiation of these policies focused on the absence of a suitable educational and organizational framework that would guarantee success. It was charged that the reform dictates were realistically unworkable with the organizational system as it currently existed.

Thus, it was that the second wave came into existence with a call not for changing policies but for changing the very structure of schools themselves. The second wave of reform with its emphasis on restructuring was typified by *School Leadership: A Preface for Action* (1988), the Carnegie Forum report, *A Nation Prepared: Teachers for the 21st Century* (1986), and *Tomorrow's Teachers* (1986) by the Holmes Group. Murphy (1990) indicated that the areas of "(1) the professionalization of teaching, (2) the development of decentralized school management systems, and (3) the enactment of specific reform topics . . . (such as programs for at-risk students" (p. 28) were the primary focus of the second wave of reform. This second surge began in 1986 and provided the impetus for site based management, teacher empowerment, and the development of school-business partnerships.

The essential problem with this round of the current reform movement is that many have misunderstood its goals. The initial surge of reform was much easier to accept with its programmatic goals of long school years and days, extensive monitoring, and higher standards. The second wave which essentially required the development of new relationships, new power structures, and extensive change has been more difficult to develop. Many schools, for instance, indicate that they utilize site based management strategies but a close scrutiny of practice finds only the establishment of more committees and task forces to study inane problems and recommend solutions that are often ignored or diluted. The concept of teacher empowerment is feared by many administrators because of the issue of control and is avoided or supported by teachers depending on their personal or political philosophies.

If this second wave of reform is to succeed, more must understand it and accept it. The attempt at restructuring and empowerment attempts to create change from the bottom up while the first wave sought change by dictating from the top down. Both have had some success but perhaps there is an additional possibility for reform.

Interestingly, Murphy (1990) indicated that the educational reform movement has now entered a third wave which focuses "directly on children" (p. 29). Table I provides an overview of the three waves Murphy envisioned. Others have yet to fully support his contention. The problem perhaps lies in the very fact that the attention should have been on children all along. Whether the emphasis is on policies, teachers, organizational structure, or administrators, the bottom line should have always been whether reform improved the educational opportunities of children. Instead, it appears that the reform movement has accepted too enthusiastically the industrial model where the end product is all that matters. The paradox that exists becomes readily evident when the product (the student) should be an educated young adult able to read, write, and effectively follow directions in the business community yet also be creatively individualistic. It is still to be determined if both attributes can coexist within the same end product.

The question that has never been satisfactorily answered throughout the reform movement and its waves is what are we as a nation really trying to accomplish? What is the vision of what schools should be? Once the vision has been collectively accepted, then how is it to be actualized? Is restructuring, redesigning, empowering or any of the myriad of other ideas the answer to the complex issue of school improvement? Perhaps the problem with this, and other reform efforts, has been the proverbial cart before the horse. Without a cogent vision is this reform all for nothing?

Certainly, the reasons that the reform movement could fail are legend. If nothing else, previous reform efforts that have accomplished substantively little should provide a word of caution and concern. Obvious constraints such as the inadequate financing of schools, the embedded bureaucracy, the intransigent organizational culture, and the fact that education becomes a political football each election year all lend themselves to the argument that this reform attempt, like so many others, will be only moderately successful.

If one seeks some consolation from the pessimism expressed above, it must be in the fact that this reform movement has endured longer than most. Certainly, there is some truth to the belief that the longer it lasts, the more institutionalized its reforms will become. Obviously, this means that the reforms will eventually become entrenched in the organizational system and its bureaucratic norms, but that in itself is the purpose of the movement. Additional support for the eventual success of the reform movement can be found in the results of some of the earlier efforts such as improved test scores, indicating to some extent strengthened student learning. The movement has also provided a better understanding of the

Table I
COMPARING THE DIFFERENT WAVES OF EDUCATIONAL
REFORM IN THE 1980s

	Wave 1	*Wave 2*	*Wave 3*
Metaphor	Fix the old clunker (repair)	Get a new car (restructure)	Rethink view of transportation (redesign)
Philosophy	Expand centralized controls	Empower professionals and parents	Empower students
Assumptions	Problems traceable to low standards for workers and low quality of production tools	Problems traceable to systems failure	Problems traceable to fragmented, uncoordinated approaches for taking care of children
Change model	Top-down (bureaucratic model)	Bottom-up (market model); lateral (professional model)	Interorganizational (interprofessional model)
Policy mechanisms	Prescription (rule making and incentives); performance measurement	Power distribution	
Focus	The system; incremental improvement	The people (professionals and parents); radical change	The child; revolutionary change
Areas	Specific pieces of quantitative requirements-standards	Governance and work structures	Delivery structure

From Joseph Murphy "Educational Reform Movement of the 1980's © 1990 by McCutchen Publishing Corporation, Berkley, CA 94702. Permission granted by the publisher.

relationship between teacher and administrator and education and the community.

Clearly, the reform movement is not over. The movement continues to expand and refocus. The first wave provided policy and curricular mandates, while the second addressed teachers and their involvement in the educational process at a variety of levels. Both waves, if one accepts the two wave standard, focused extensively on what changes occurred in public schools, teaching, and student learning. Recently, there has been a realization that in much of the early reform school administrators were essentially ignored and placed in the roles of agents or enforcers of the reform. The renewed attention to administrators has primarily focused on their preparation by institutions of higher education, as it became apparent that administrators were an integral component in the reform effort and could mightily impact its success or failure.

REFORM AND ADMINISTRATOR PREPARATION

The national reform movement, until recently, had been only obliquely interested and concerned about administrators and administrator preparation programs. Early warnings of criticism (Achilles, 1984; Peterson & Finn, 1985) primarily were concerned with the methodology utilized by many universities to train prospective administrators. As time passed, it became abundantly clear that any true reform must have the support and consent of school administrators. Without that support, reform measures could be subverted or weakened by leaders who had little commitment or concern for the success of the reforms.

The publication of *Leaders for America's Schools* (1987) was the first major attempt to identify deficiencies and recommend viable reform policies. This work, sponsored by the University Council for Educational Administration (UCEA), advanced several postulates. These included but were not limited to:

1. The establishment of a National Policy Board for Educational Administration.
2. The notion that administrator preparation programs should adopt the professional school model utilized by law and medicine.
3. The supposition that too many higher education institutions prepared administrators and this diluted preparation programs. They therefore recommended that many small universities and colleges should withdraw from preparing administrators.
4. The call for a significant increase in the number of women and minorities admitted to preparation programs. This was deemed necessary in order to more fully reflect the multicultural diversity of society.
5. The belief that certification requirements should be substantially improved and expanded.

6. The proposal that those higher education institutions which retained preparation programs should develop extensive partnerships with public schools so that administrator training could be significantly improved (p. xiii).

This report caused a tremendous hue and cry from the smaller colleges across the country which avowed that they provided a more pragmatic education for administrators than did the larger, more research oriented universities. Very few institutions responded by eliminating preparation programs. Indeed, many expanded their programs or developed new training models in response to the significant number of retirements among practicing administrators across the country. Amazingly, the recommendation for establishing a National Policy Board provoked very little discussion or criticism.

The National Policy Board for Educational Administration (NPB) was established with the financial support of the Danforth Foundation, the UCEA, and other administrator-related professional organizations. These organizations included groups such as the American Association for School Administrators, the National Association of Elementary School Principals, the National Association of Secondary School Principals, the Association for Supervision and Curriculum Development, and the American Association of Colleges for Teacher Education. The NPB was initially situated at the University of Virginia.

In 1989 the NPB released their reform agenda. The relatively brief list of recommendations titled *Improving the Preparation of School Administrators: An Agenda for Reform* immediately created a storm of debate. Many of the professional organizations that had supported the establishment of the NPB instantly disavowed some of the report's recommendations.

The report advanced nine proposals focused around three broad categories. These categories addressed the issue of people/personnel, programmatic concerns and needs, and the question of assessment. Several of the more debated recommendations were:

1. That entrance requirements and standards for administrator preparation programs should be significantly increased;
2. That each university's administrator preparation program have a critical number of qualified faculty which was deemed to be at least five;
3. That the doctorate in educational administration (Ed.D.) be a mandatory prerequisite for certification as a school administrator;

4. That individuals who desired to become school administrators be required to complete one year of full-time residency as well as a year of full-time field-based residency;
5. That a common curriculum and unified knowledge base be agreed upon for all administrator preparation programs;
6. That long-term working relationships be established between public schools and universities for purposes of service and research;
7. That administrator preparation programs establish a plan to vigorously recruit women and minorities; and,
8. That national accreditation and a national professional standards board become the method by which quality assurance of programs and people be guaranteed (p. 5–7).

These recommendations caused exactly what they were intended, and that was an intense dialogue within the higher education community and among administrator professional organizations. The reform movement had finally addressed administrator preparation and it seemed that the reform discussion had been much more palatable when it was focused on policy or teachers rather than on administrators.

In October, 1989, the University Council for Educational Administration, one of the charter members in the two previously discussed reports, issued its own document regarding administrator preparation programs. This short one page position paper, *The Preparation of Educational Administrators* (1989), diluted some of the more controversial stands of the other two reports while reiterating those which seemed too innoculous and acceptable to all concerned. A few of the UCEA recommendations were:

1. That a relevant knowledge base for school administrators be established;
2. That each potential administrator participate in periods of intense concentrated study as well as be provided the opportunity for clinical practice;
3. That all preparation programs be required to maintain a critical mass of faculty;
4. That recruitment programs should focus on women, minorities, and educators who have been exceptionally successful; and,
5. That the completion of a master degree be a prerequisite for entrance into all administrator preparation programs (p. 1).

Clearly, this position statement supported many of the NPB's recommendations while homogenizing the more controversial ones.

The response to the concerns of administrator preparation has been similar to that exhibited in the early days of the reform movement. The reaction to concerns expressed in 1983–1984 was the development of top down policy mandates. Concerns over the quality of administrators and university preparation programs have resulted in top down responses relating to certification and residency requirements. It remains to be seen if these reactions centering around policy mandates can move further into the concept of leadership development. Preparatory programs cannot improve by dictating more sameness, but rather must focus on the uniqueness of the individual and the need for proactive leaders who hold a viable vision of what education should be for all children.

CONCLUSION

Since 1983 the country has been struggling with the issue of reform. The movement began initially by addressing policy concerns and then focused on the role of the teacher by championing shared decision making and site-based management as part of the restructuring process. By the end of the decade, it was obvious that any true reform would happen only if administrators in the schools were willing to assume the role of leader first and manager second.

As the reform debate began to focus on administrator preparation, it became evident that programmatic changes were necessary in higher education preparation programs in order to change how schools function. Any reform effort would ultimately fail, be it from top down or bottom up, without the support of administrators in schools. This meant school administrators must become leaders who were part of the solution and not part of the problem. This mandated that school administrators must proactively and cooperatively work with all concerned to improve schools. In order to accomplish this, administrators first must know where they were going and how to get there. The reform movement must have visionary leaders in order to succeed.

Chapter II

AN OVERVIEW OF SCHOOL LEADERSHIP AND ADMINISTRATIVE DEVELOPMENT

The reform movement, or any attempt at improving schools, will fail without the support of school administrators. If anything since the publication of *The Nation at Risk* (1983), it has become clear that change is difficult to accomplish in a system that by its very nature is designed to maintain the status quo.

Although the reform movement is not over, its efforts to date have been very useful in refocusing the mission of public education. Despite the fact that this is important, the reality remains that any widespread success depends upon the quality of leadership manifested in schools in this country (Blumberg & Greenfield, 1980; Brookover, Beady, Hood, Schweitzer, & Wisenbaker, 1975; Edmonds, 1979; Sweeney, 1982). There is a strong positive relationship between an effective administrator and the ability of the school to accomplish established goals and objectives regardless of whether they are developed at the state, district, or building level (Guthrie & Reed, 1986; Leithwood & Montgomery, 1982; Lipham, 1981; Manasse, 1985).

Educational studies have stressed the importance for administrators to possess both long- and short-term goals, educational objectives, and a well-thought-out philosophy (Leithwood & Montgomery, 1982; Manasse, 1985; Russell, Maggarella, White & Maurer, 1985; Stallings & Mohlman, 1981; Sergiovanni, 1987; Sweeney, 1982). These attributes, among others, have been identified as significant characteristics of effective leaders. However, most school administrators, indoctrinated in behavioral sciences and classical theory, are not prepared to be leaders but rather are trained to be managers. Even though the knowledge base exists for administrators to utilize, too often they become enmeshed in the bureaucratic nature of schools where rules, compliance, and support of the system is the norm (Weick, 1982).

This chapter discusses the concept of leadership, the historical devel-

13

opment of administrative theory, various theoretical approaches that have influenced administrators and affected preparation programs, and concludes with a review of new leadership theories that can facilitate school improvement.

LEADERSHIP

Defining leadership is not an easy task. Some adhere to the belief that leaders are born; some that they are created. All leaders are not the same. Some leaders are despots, others humanitarians. The real mystery is what makes one individual a leader and another one not, when both have similar attributes, abilities, and situations. Definitions of leadership and leadership theories abound. The following definitions will serve only as a starting place for the discussion of leadership and leaders.

> Leaders are people who are able to express themselves fully.... They know who they are, what their strengths and weaknesses are, and how to fully deploy their strengths and compensate for their weaknesses. They know what they want, why they want it, and how to communicate what they want to others, in order to gain their cooperation and support (Bennis, 1989, p. 3).

> Leadership is the initiation of a new structure for accomplishing an organization's goals and objectives . . . (Lipham, 1964, p. 122).

> Challenging the process, inspiring a shared vision, enabling others to act, modeling the way, and encouraging the heart: these are the practices that leaders use to get extraordinary things done in organizations (Kouzes & Posner, 1987, p. 15).

> Leadership is the process of influencing the activities of an organized group toward goal setting and achievement (Stogdill, 1950, p. 4).

> The essence of organizational leadership is the influential increment over and above mechanical compliance with the routine directives of the organization (Katz & Kahn, 1987, p. 528).

> Leadership is many things. It is patient, usually boring coalition building.... It's listening carefully much of the time, frequently speaking with encouragement, and reinforcing words with believable action (Peters & Waterman, 1982, p. 82).

> ... Leadership is a cult, a religion, and we persist in our dreams that great leaders will emerge and become our salvation ... this is as it should be, for our future welfare depends on our hopes, aspirations, and dreams of what might be possible with great leadership (Blumberg & Greenfield, 1986, p. 232).

> ... Charismatic leaders are unique in their ability to build emotional attachment and enthusiasm among their followers or themselves and their missions (Conger & Kanungo, 1988, p. 4).

Leadership in organizations involves the exercise of authority and the making of decisions (Dubin, 1968, p. 385).

Leaders are people who do the right thing; managers are people who do things right. Both roles are crucial but they differ profoundly (Bennis, 1989, p. 18).

Definitions of leadership are not uniform but have some common aspects relating to the accomplishment of goals, the interaction of people, or ascribed characteristics. Katz and Kahn (1978) identified three common aspects of leadership. These were an attribute of an office, a characteristic of a person, and a type of actual behavior (p. 517–518). Leadership involves followers because there can be no leaders without those who support and follow them. Leadership reflects power and how it is used to gain compliance, acceptance, influence, or more power.

The concept of leadership sounds somewhat elusive. However, most are able to recognize a good leader. This is often a result of each individual's needs and perceptions as he/she views someone as a potential leader. In truth, both the definition and the recognition of a leader often are dependent upon the nature of the organization, its structure, and various goals and objectives. In schools, those who control or maintain order are often viewed as leaders by teachers and the public. But this does not necessarily make them effective leaders. Principals and superintendents are leaders not due to their position or control, but because of the manner in which they exercise their influence and power. School leaders must represent a proactive model, not the maintenance of the status quo.

HISTORICAL BACKGROUND OF ADMINISTRATION

The type of leadership exhibited in schools is crucial to their success. This does not mean that administrators have been prepared to be leaders. The very nature of the word administrator often leads to the conclusion that this refers to management. Preparation programs for school administrators often concern themselves with managerial activities to the exclusion of leadership ones. This management orientation has been an integral component of programs, and often theories, for many years. The science of preparing school administrators has evolved in three phases or stages. The evolutionary process is not concluded, and indeed, must continue if school administrators are to effectively lead the educational system of the 21st century. A review of the three stages is important if one is to understand the process that brought preparation programs to their current place. The three stages are the classical organizational theory period, the human relations movement, and the current, albeit paling, behavioral science period.

Classical Organizational Theory

The classical organizational theory period was epitomized by the work of Frederick Taylor (1856–1915) who is often referred to as the father of scientific management. Taylor's concepts were expressed in his 1911 work *The Principles of Scientific Management.* Taylor viewed workers in much the same manner as industrialists of the period contemplated machinery and the assembly process. The basic notions of Taylor and his followers, often referred to as human engineers, were:

1. There must be a hierarchical chain of command with various levels of authority and an established division of labor;
2. Each individual in the organization must have a clearly defined task;
3. There should be well established rules of behavior and a system of punishments that are personally costly if one violates the rules or fails to complete the assigned task;
4. Workers must be recruited on the basis of their ability and technical knowledge;
5. Employees should be expected to perform the task in a like manner since all tasks have been standardized.

Taylor believed his ideas would result in each and every job being performed efficiently and with the least effort.

Taylor's scientific management approach was adapted by other classical organizational theorists such as Henri Fayol and Luther Gulick. These two reinforced the philosophy that workers must be constantly directed and controlled by management. Because of this principle, good leaders understood the need for a formal bureaucratic organization. Hoy and Miskel (1982) indicate that classical organizational theory tenets are best represented by the following:

1. Time and Motion Studies. Is a task carried out in a way that minimizes time and effort required?
2. Division of labor and Specialization. Efficiency can be attained by subdividing any operation into its basic components to ensure workers' performance.

3. Standardization of Tasks. Breaking tasks into component parts allows for routinized performance.
4. Unity of Command. To coordinate the organization, decision making is centralized, with responsibility flowing from top to bottom.
5. Span of Control. Unity of command and coordination are possible only if each superior at any level has a limited number of subordinates (five to ten) to direct.
6. Uniqueness of Function. One department of an organization should not duplicate the function performed by another.
7. Formal Organization. The focus of analysis is on the official organizational blueprint; semiformal and informal structures created by the dynamic interaction within the formal organization are not analyzed (p. 4–5).

Many school administrators labor under the precepts of the classical organizational theorists. They believe that control flowing downward from the superintendent is the only means by which to function. Testing of students, evaluation of teachers, and curriculum guidelines are important because they measure the completion of tasks and maintain the scientific standard of differentiated work. There is a strong support for the maintenance of a division of labor as teachers and students are pigeonholed into their areas of expertise and ability. Full acceptance and support of rules and regulations is mandated by policies found in the faculty or student handbook. A failure to abide by the rules and other norms of behavior results in a disciplinary process. Finally, administrators, and teachers, continually seek the one best way to accomplish the task of educating students in the least amount of time and with the least amount of effort. Clearly, it is no small wonder that schools find it difficult to change since the very organizational structure lends itself to classical organizational theory where the school factory manufactures a finished product of an educated youth.

Human Relations Period

The notion that workers were content to be viewed impersonally and as components of an assembly process came under attack in the 1930s with the work of Mary Parker Follett, Elton Mayo, and Fritz Roethlisberger. These three, and others, espoused the concept that people work harder when treated well. This approach came to be called the human relations approach. Many of the concepts expressed in this period were a result of studies conducted at the Hawthorne Plant owned by the Western Electric Company. The series of experiments conducted at the Hawthorne plant provided the basis for the assertion that people are motivated by the manner in which they are treated and made to feel important more than through economic incentives or coercive threats.

The studies concluded that although a well developed formal organization may exist, it is the informal organization with a multitude of interpersonal interactions, informal leaders, and a system of unwritten social norms that is often the most powerful organizational element. This informal organization can impact productivity substantially more than a chain of command, specialized tasks, or superordinate control. The human relations period provided school administrators with the knowledge that employees work harder and more productively when satisfied and respected. The human relations approach failed to immediately gain a great degree of support.

There are several reasons for this, partly related to the power of scientific management devotees but also because of the economic and political climate of the nation during the Depression. Schools and school administrators were well engrained in the tenets of classical organizational theory. Those administrators who did elect to incorporate motivational and interpersonal strategies into their schools were also the ones who more readily accepted other new ideas such as the life adjustment curriculum which emphasized individual needs and human diversity.

The human relations approach would not come into its own until the late 1940s when the study of human relations became an accepted academic field. It also would reappear in the behavioral science period as a component of contingency and situational leadership theories which advocated the importance of quality human relationships and their impact on task completion.

Behavioral Science Phase

The behavioral science approach has been the accepted theoretical base for administration since the publication of Barnard's *The Function of the Executive* (1938). Behavioral science undertakes to include ideas and constructs from the social sciences, i.e., sociology, psychology, political science, economics, and history. Although the full impact of this multidimensional approach would not be fully evident until the 1950s and

1960s, the essential concepts are reflected in a better understanding of how schools function.

The behavioral science phase provides a more acceptable scientific approach to the study of schools and administrators. Theoretical, empirical research and extensive analysis of collected data, both descriptive and causal, became the accepted operational norm. The result is that the quality of theoretical knowledge regarding leadership, formal and informal organizational structures, human interactions, and administrative approaches has improved and expanded.

It may very well be that as a theoretical construct the behavioral science phase has been more useful for university researchers than for school practitioners. The dissemination of information concerning the role of the bureaucracy, schools as social systems, and the interaction of the social sciences in the concept of logical positivism has done little to change or improve either schools or the leadership found in them. Certainly, the behavioral science period has expanded the theoretical and knowledge base concerning administration, but in many cases this did not assist the practitioner (Culbertson, 1985; Griffiths, 1989; Halpin, 1960). The primary problem with theories advanced through the behavioral science approach is the attempt to simplify human interaction and behavior to a state of predictability that is often unrealistic and irrational (Foster, 1980; Greenfield, 1975).

Administrative theory is at a crossroads today as few of the old constructs which viewed the roles of administrators and how they act/react within the confines of the educational institution provide adequate predictions of results. Perhaps, it is time to seek new answers to a new set of questions and problems that have become increasingly complex. The answers will come if administrators in schools attempt to develop a new leadership approach for dealing with people and the organization. But before a new approach can be developed and utilized, it is important to review the various leadership theories that have provided the current conceptualization of leadership.

LEADERSHIP THEORIES AND APPROACHES

The debate has long existed over how leaders become leaders. Through the mid 1940s many accepted the idea that good leaders exhibited certain characteristics and that leaders were born with these as a result of genetic predilection. A second set of beliefs, emerging in the early 1950s, supported the viewpoint that the situation controlled the possibility of becoming a leader. A third view of leadership advanced the construct that it was a combination of abilities and characteristics as well as the place in time or situation that impacted one's leadership aptitude. The first assumption of leadership development is best known as the trait approach; the second organizational environmental; and, the third set of postulates contingency or situational approaches.

Trait Approaches

The trait approach to leadership supports the view that some individuals are born to be leaders. Historically, Thomas Carlyle (1795–1881) proposed the great man in history concept. This theory expressed the philosophy that some people are simply born to lead and through that leadership impact the history of mankind. Because of political and social events of the mid to late 1800s, this thesis fit well into other philosophies such as Social Darwinism with its concept of survival of the fittest.

It was a simple process to move from a great man in history theory to a compilation of specific leadership traits that allowed some to succeed while others failed. The most noted work in trait leadership theory was conducted by Stogdill (1948, 1974) who reviewed over 300 trait related studies. Stogdill found that although there was some evidence that effective leaders often exhibited certain characteristics, there was no consistent pattern that could lead to solid irrefutable conclusions as to those traits that impacted one's ability to lead.

Stogdill did identify in his 1948 study certain general leadership factors that appeared as possible traits. He categorized these into five broad areas. They were:

1. Capacity. This referred to intelligence, judgment, originality, and verbal ability;
2. Achievement. The traits in this area are primarily scholarship and knowledge;
3. Responsibility. Persistence, confidence, dependability, and initiative are the traits exhibited in this category;
4. Participation. Sociability and cooperation are the two primary traits; and,
5. Status. One's socioeconomic status as well as likability are important traits relating to status (Stogdill, 1948).

The 1974 study determined that some of the same traits as ascertained in the 1948 study were still of potential significance. Table II represents the basic traits and skills that Stogdill indicates are most likely to be characteristics of successful leaders.

Table II
TRAITS AND SKILLS FOUND MOST FREQUENTLY TO BE
CHARACTERISTIC OF SUCCESSFUL LEADERS

Traits	*Skills*
Adaptable to situations	Clever (intelligent)
Alert to social environment	Conceptually skilled
Ambitious and achievement-oriented	Creative
Assertive	Diplomatic and tactful
Cooperative	Fluent in speaking
Decisive	Knowledgeable about group task
Dependable	Organized (administrative ability)
Dominant (desire to influence others)	Persuasive
Energetic (high activity level)	Socially skilled
Persistent	
Self-confident	
Tolerant of stress ·	
Willing to assume responsibility	

Gary A. Yukl, Leadership in Organizations 2e, © 1989, pp. 176. Reprinted by permission of Prentice Hall, Inc., Englewood Cliffs, New Jersey.

The trait approach to leadership when strictly applied presupposes that leaders are born and are an accident of genetics. The tendency is to dismiss the approach because of these assertions. However, certain traits that are evident in effective leaders cannot be discarded as simplistic rhetoric. There is a kernel of truth in the trait approach. The recognition of these traits when combined with other elements is useful. The effective school movement has identified certain characteristics of effective administrators. This represents a semitrait approach. Bennis and Nanus (1985), in their thought provoking discussion of leaders, were able to isolate certain common managerial and leadership traits in the ninety leaders in their study. As a final note, traits are not always positive but may be highly negative and counterproductive given the right set of circumstances. The recognition and reinforcement of positive attributes among school administrators should be a goal of university preparation programs as well as staff development.

Organizational Environmental Approach

The organizational environmental approach, or sometimes referred to as a situational approach, developed as a reaction to the trait approach to leadership. Succinctly stated, the organizational environmental approach infers that certain variables found in each situation or organizational setting impact on the ability of an individual to lead. Variables that have been identified by Hoy and Miskel (1982) in such situations are:

1. Structural properties of the organization (size, hierarchical structure, formalization);
2. Organizational climate (openness, participativeness, group atmosphere);
3. Role characteristics (position power, type and difficulty of task, procedural rules);
4. Subordinate characteristics (knowledge and experience, tolerance for ambiguity, responsibility, power) (p. 223).

Many theorists also discuss the organizational environmental approach but identify this as a combination of both leadership traits, the role of subordinates, the organization, external and internal organizational constraints and variables, and role expectations and requirements. There is very little evidence to support the concept that leaders primarily exist based upon the type of organization and the situation. This short-lived view of leadership has given way to a broader definition which included the aspects of personality, organizational factors, and the situation. This broader definition falls under the general rubric of contingency approaches to leadership.

Contingency Approaches to Leadership

The contingency approach combined the basic tenets of the trait approach with that of the organizational situation. This creates a multitude of variables, thus establishing that no single leadership approach to a problem is the complete and only answer. Different leaders given the same situation under various circumstances will respond in a dissimilar manner. Each and every one of those responses could be successful. The contingency approach implies that a leader must be flexible and willing to develop a diverse repertory of actions, reactions, and behaviors.

Contingency approaches to leadership include but are not limited to Fiedler's Leadership Contingency Model (1971), House's Path Goal Theory (1971), Vroom and Yetten's Contingency or Normative Model (1973), and Hersey and Blanchard's Situational Leadership Model (1988). In all of these, the leader's individual personal attributes, abilities, and skills are utilized in relationship to the subordinate's willingness and abilities. Constraints such as time, the task, organizational goals, and the use of power interact with the style of the leader and the subordinate. This multirelationship infers that a leader must do an analysis of the total situation before acting and carefully select an appropriate leadership response. In reality, this simply does not take place. But inherent in these theories is the belief that a leader can develop an assortment of appropriate styles of behavior and learn to be more flexible in choosing a leadership response.

Fiedler's Approach

Fiedler's Leadership Contingency Model (1967) examined the relationship between leadership traits and interpersonal motivation, leadership actions and behaviors, and the situation. Fiedler developed an instrument determining personality traits. This instrument given to an organization's leader would have him/her score the least preferred coworker in the organization. The Least Preferred Coworker (LPC) scale allowed the leader to rate the person in question by selecting between bipolar paired adjectives which are extreme opposites. An example would be cooperative/uncooperative or efficient/inefficient. The more critically one responds regarding the least preferred coworker, the lower is the resultant LPC score. Conversely, if one scores high when rating the least preferred coworker then the implication is that the leader is more motivated to resolve differences and develop viable relationships with a difficult coworker. The leader who scores high on the LPC in effect indicates the desire to develop a harmonious environment even with the least preferred subordinates. It follows that a low LPC score signifies less concern for the work environment and employee relationships. It implies that task completion takes precedence over relationships.

Fiedler indicated that the primary factor in viewing the relationships between the LPC and leader effectiveness was what he identified as situational favorableness (1971, 1976). Three major ingredients impact the degree to which a leader can function in a particular situation. These are the positional power of the leader, the relationship between organizational members of the group and the leader, and the task structure. The degree of favorability is based upon the assumption that relationships are more important than either the task or position power and that the task is more important than the position power of the leader. Thus, relationships followed by task and then positional power form a type of hierarchy.

The result of these assumptions is the development of eight levels or octants of favorability. Octant one represents the best possible combination of situational variables and, conversely, octant eight represents the poorest situational variable. Given this type of structure, favorability is highest when leader relationships are good with subordinates, the task is structured, and the leader has a high degree of power. Obviously, octant eight would find the opposite of all of these variables.

A final element of Fiedler's Model is that there is a direct relationship between scores on the LPC, which represent how leaders view others, and the need for a harmonious relationship or the completion of a set task and the situational favorability factors. Thus, the effectiveness of a leader is a result of the interplay between situational favorability factors such as task structure, position power, and superordinate-subordinate relations and the score received on the LPC. Fiedler envisions leader effectiveness quite narrowly. A leader is effective if the group accomplishes its primary task, ineffective if it does not.

If task completion is judged as the measure of leader effectiveness, then clearly low LPC rated leaders are more effective at the extremes of the models. A low relationship score and leader at octant one will have a negligible impact on the task completion since the situational favorability is so high. At octant eight, a leader will need to be highly directive since the situational favorability is poor and thus a low LPC score indicates the directiveness needed. A leader who scores high on the LPC with his/her concern about relationships will be more effective in octants four through seven where the situational favorability factors are more moderate.

The Fiedler Contingency Model was the first major effort which attempted to identify leader effectiveness as the relationship between a number of situational variables and certain leadership characteristics. If the theory behind the model is valid, then schools would be best served by matching those with certain LPC leadership scores to schools that exhibit certain situational favorability variables. Thus, more directive and task-oriented leaders would be placed in schools at both high and low extremes, while relationship-oriented administrators would do better in average or moderate schools. Fiedler's work is important because it postulated leadership style as directly related to leader motivation and leader effectiveness is the result of an interaction between leader style and situational variables.

Path-Goal Theory

Path-Goal Theory as formulated by House (1971) and later modified by House and Mitchell (1974) is a situational approach that identifies how leaders influence subordinates' efforts and goal attainment. This theory is a direct outgrowth of the Ohio State studies and expectancy theory. It postulates that there are four distinct leadership behaviors. These are directive, supporting, participative, and achievement-oriented. Simply put, a directive leader establishes firm expectations, rules, and procedures while providing very specific guidance. A supportive leader displays concern for subordinates and acknowledges their needs by creating a harmonious work environment. Participative leaders actively interact with subordinates in a consultative manner. An achievement-oriented leader emphasizes excellence as a performance goal and exhibits a high degree of confidence that subordinates will achieve established goals.

The theory also identifies two situational variables. These are the diverse characteristics of the subordinates and the nature of the task within the work environment. A subordinate's perception of his/her ability is important because the greater the perception of ability then less direction and guidance needs to be given by the superordinate to the subordinate. Those with high perceptions of ability will find it difficult to effectively work with highly directive leaders. A second characteristic pertains to how each subordinate views the degree of control he/she has as an individual over the work environment. Each subordinate either perceives that he/she has some control or that he/she does not.

The term work environment refers to factors not traditionally controlled by subordinates such as the nature of the task, organizational norms, and the manner in which authority is employed in the environment or system. The level of control perceived directly influences the successful completion of tasks.

Path-Goal Theory is a situational approach to leadership because it defines and identifies leader effectiveness to the extent that subordinate motivation increases, job satisfaction improves, and the leader is more fully accepted by subordinates. The situational construct relates to how well a leader chooses one of the four leader behaviors and is able to motivate subordinates or influence their perception of the task and organizational goals. Obviously, certain leader behaviors are best for structured tasks and certain behaviors are better suited for unstructured tasks. The key in the Path-Goal Theory is the ability of the leader to select an appropriate leadership orientation in order to facilitate subordinate psychological growth and a more motivated work effort.

Vroom-Yetten Contingency Normative Model

The Vroom-Yetten Contingency Model (1973) basically hypothesizes that organizational effectiveness is a direct result of the interaction of a variety of situational variables with certain identifiable personal characteristics and attributes of a leader. The model accentuates the role of the leader in decision making and asserts that the quality of the decision and the level of acceptance by subordinates serves as a direct causal factor pertaining to job performance and organizational effectiveness.

Vroom and Yetten developed a decision model matrix composed of five distinctly different, decision-oriented managerial styles. These styles range from a leader who solves the problem by deciding unilaterally to the style where the subordinates generate solutions and arrive at a solution through participatory consensus. The model also utilizes a series of diagnostic questions which address the structure of the problem, the quality of leader-held information, and probable conflict avoidance solutions. The decision matrix allows a leader to ascertain the type of response necessary in a given situation (Fig. 1).

The model is quite simple to use. It is dependent upon the quality of the response provided by the leader at each step of the decision matrix. The response to each step is also colored by the leader's perceptions of reality and his/her level of useful knowledge. The model serves as a good example of the situational or contingency approach because it addresses specific behaviors that will result in specific probable outcomes.

Hersey-Blanchard Situational Leadership Model

The Situational Leadership Model developed by Hersey and Blanchard (1988) has several similarities to models designed by Blake and Mouton (1964) and Reddin (1970). Similarities in the models are the use of the

Figure 1. Decision Process Flowchart (Feasible Set).

A. Does the problem possess a quality requirement?
B. Do I have sufficient information to make a high-quality decision?
C. Is the problem structured?
D. Is acceptance of the decision by subordinates important for effective implementation?
E. If I were to make the decision by myself, am I reasonably certain that it would be accepted by my subordinates?
F. Do subordinates share the organizational goals to be attained in solving this problem?
G. Is conflict among subordinates likely in preferred solutions?

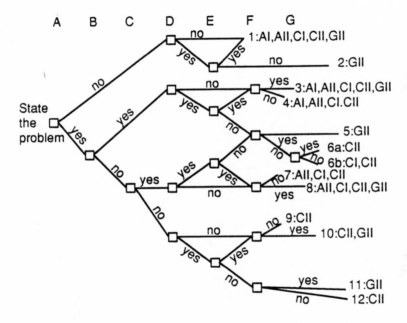

two dimensions of task or production and relationship to individuals. The Hersey-Blanchard Model added a third dimension relating to the readiness level of subordinates. Earlier versions of the model referred to readiness as maturity.

Hersey and Blanchard (1988) define task behavior as "the extent to which the leader engages in spelling out the duties and responsibilities of an individual or group" (p. 172). The level of task behavior can be high or low depending upon the level of reaction expected from subordinates. They further indicate that "task behavior is characterized by one way communication from the leader to the follower" (p. 172). Relationship behavior refers to the degree of interpersonal skills such as supporting and facilitating as well as to the degree of two-way communication. The two dimensions of task and relationship are formulated into a four quadrant model with task displayed from low to high on a horizontal axis and relationship from low to high on a vertical axis.

The four quadrants represent four leadership styles best identified as telling, selling, participating, and delegating. Each leadership style denotes the degree of interaction between relationship and task. For instance, quadrant one, telling, represents a high concern for task completion and a low concern for interpersonal relationships. Each quadrant indicates a similar leadership style representative of the interaction between task and relationship.

The third dimension of the Hersey and Blanchard Model is the readiness or maturity level of subordinates. Readiness refers to the extent to which a subordinate is willing and able to successfully accomplish a specific organizational task. Ability is defined as "the knowledge, experience, and skill that an individual or group brings to a particular task or activity" (Hersey and Blanchard, 1988, p. 175). They also describe willingness as referring to "the extent to which an individual or group has the confidence, commitment, and motivation to accomplish a specific task" (p. 175). Thus, ability is whether one can complete the task; willingness is whether one has the desire to do so.

Four readiness levels are identified, ranging from low to moderate to high. Each of the four levels reflects a combination of some degree of willingness and ability. Thus, one may range from unable and unwilling to able, willing, and confident. Since a subordinate, or follower, may fall at any of the levels, a goal of each leader is to move a subordinate to a higher, more effective and efficient level by coaching, guiding, and providing success opportunities. Each readiness level corresponds to one of the four quadrants of task and relationship, i.e., leadership style.

The total model matches the subordinate readiness level with a leadership style so the task can be accomplished, relationships can be maintained, and follower abilities and willingness improves. Altogether, it is essentially a matching of quadrants and styles. A subordinate at a low readiness level (R1) would be more successful, at least initially, working with a leader who utilized a telling style of leadership characterized by a high task structure with a low concern for relationship. A subordinate at the R1 level needs more guidance and direction so the task can be successfully completed. As more tasks are completed, and skills and confidence increase on the part of the subordinate, then the leader can begin to move to other styles of leadership.

In the same vein as the above example, if the subordinate is an R1, unable and unwilling, and the leader elects to use a leadership style of delegating, S4, represented by low task and low relationship behavior, it is obvious that the subordinate will not in all probability be successful. A subordinate in this scenario has no opportunity to improve his/her readiness level and the leader will be unhappy because the task was not completed.

Hersey and Blanchard (1988) have also developed a series of instruments that purport to determine the levels of readiness of subordinates, styles of leadership for managers, and the best match between readiness and leadership style. This is not meant to imply that the Situational Leadership Model has discovered the secret to all leadership needs. Even Hersey and Blanchard (1988) state, "Situational Leadership is not a prescription with hard and fast rules. . . . Situational Leadership is a major contribution. . . . is attempting to improve the odds" (p. 180–181).

The emphasis on flexibility makes the Situational Leadership Model a viable tool for leaders. Its tridimensional approach takes into account the importance of matching leadership behavior to subordinate maturity and readiness. Although the model has been criticized for its absence of a research base (Graeff, 1983; Yukl, 1989), it is quite popular among business executives and school administrators. Perhaps that is because of the relative simplicity of the model or because it makes sense to those who elect to utilize it. Whatever the case, Situational Leadership is one of the most widely accepted models by practitioners. The acknowledgement that leaders can learn to employ different approaches with different subordinates as a response to a subordinate's job readiness is an important and powerful tool for leaders.

LEADERSHIP FOR IMPROVING SCHOOLS

Educational administration and school leadership has come a long way in the past one hundred years. As evidenced by the early part of this chapter, there has been a tremendous amount of research on accomplishing organizational goals as well as managing systems and human beings.

Although much of the research has been useful, the publication of *The Nation at Risk* (1983) seemed to open the flood gates as complaints and intense criticism came from all sectors both within and outside the educational profession. One cannot help but wonder what all of the theories, models, and historical periods have given us except theories, models, and historical periods. Are schools better today? Are all children receiving a superior education? Are local communities and the business communities supportive of education? The reform impetus would indicate that the educational system in this country still has some distance to go.

This is not meant to imply that any of the research discussed has only been an exercise in intellectualism. Indeed, perhaps the problem lies in the application of the research base to the world of the practitioner. The reform movement, even through the first wave of policy and top down mandates, began to view schools and research in a different manner. That view was often more pragmatic than heretofore manifested. From that pragmatic, practitioner-oriented milieu came some new concepts and approaches that, although often viewed as less research-oriented, appear to work. Some of these are an adjunct to the general reform movement; some are an extension of the study of leadership and leadership theory.

For the purposes of this work, only two approaches will be reviewed. The first which emerged as a part of the reform process is the effective school movement. The second is a leadership approach that suggests leaders need to evolve from managers and technicians to roles which are symbolic and cultural. Sergiovanni's (1984, 1987) Forces of Leadership provides a clarion call for a new type of administrator.

This section will discuss these two different yet connected views of leadership that desire to improve schools. The effective schools approach is much more managerial-oriented; the second approach provides a basis for the development of new leadership. These two in consort with an educational organizational vision provide the foundation for true school reform and educational improvement.

The Effective School Movement

The Effective School Movement traces its inception to the work of Edmonds (1979, 1984), Rutter et al. (1979), Brookover and Lezotte (1981), and Lezotte and Bancroft (1985). The concept advanced by Edmonds

(1979) and others consists of five factors. These five correlates, so identi-fied because of the nature of their interrelationship, are (1) instructional leadership by the principal; (2) a safe, orderly school climate; (3) an instructional focus on well established academic goals; (4) high expecta-tions for student performance and achievement; and, (5) frequent, sys-tematic measurement of students to ascertain their level of performance.

The intent here is not to discuss the movement or its constructs in detail, but rather synthesize the effective school movement. In viewing effective school research, it is important to remember the interrelationship of the correlates. The successful accomplishment of any one of the elements will not provide an effective school. Only when all five are addressed, can a school hope to become more effective. If one accepts the correlates as the basis of an effective school, this does not mean that other factors also do not contribute to a school's success. Researchers (Purkey and Smith, 1982; Roueche and Baker, 1986; Stedman, 1987; Waupon, 1988) have identified several other characteristics that contribute to effectiveness.

These contributing aspects include the following:

1. A well-designed, school-wide staff development program;
2. A high degree of staff input into instructional decisions and training;
3. An accepted student-centered focus;
4. A climate exemplified by optimism and high expectations;
5. A work atmosphere personified by collegiality and empowerment;
6. An extracurricular program that serves as an adjunct to academics for enrichment purposes;
7. A milieu of student responsibility and growth;
8. An academic offering that addresses higher as well as lower order cognitive objectives;
9. A well-designed sequential and incremental curriculum with excel-lent teacher delivery skills as the norm; and,
10. An administrator who serves as an instructional leader, under-stands curriculum development, communicates appropriately, and actually delegates, empowers, and collaborates with others.

Although these serve only as additions to the five correlates, the five provide the foundation for the movement. These correlates when com-bined with other characteristics of effective schools provide for the estab-lishment of a total school culture best represented by "a structure, process, and climate of values and norms that channel staff and students in the direction of successful teaching and learning" (Purkey and Smith, 1982, p. 68). In effect, the effective school concept calls for a new approach, one in which people's behaviors and attitudes, as well as the school's organizational norms and functions undergo significant change.

Criticism of the effective school movement has come from many directions primarily because of the perceived absence of a well-established empirical research base (Cawelti, 1984; Purkey & Smith, 1982). Although this may hold some truth since much of the research is relatively new and initially was conducted in urban, inner city schools, the fact remains that the effective school movement has provided a new focus for improving schools. Some of the more relevant aspects of the movement are:

1. There must be a strong emphasis on educational objectives;
2. The role of the administrator is well defined;
3. There is a strong emphasis on the school as a place for learning;
4. Curricular goals are well defined and supported;
5. Positive teacher behaviors are exhibited to all students;
6. The total staff is actively involved in maintaining an orderly learning environment;
7. Instructional time is protected, emphasized, and deemed important;
8. There is a low level of employee turnover and relatively high employee morale;
9. Administrators use their power in a positive manner;
10. Administrators establish, support, and reinforce the overall sense of involvement in the school;
11. Administrators focus on the quality of instruction;
12. There is a self reinforcing cycle of normative behavior in the school.

The desire to create an effective school requires a great deal of hard work and total commitment to the educational process by all involved. The research appears to place most of the emphasis on the role of the principal as the instructional leader (Behling & Champion, 1984; Dwyer, 1986; Hallinger & Murphy, 1985; Sweeney, 1982).

This emphasis on the principal as leader requires a new approach to the role. The concept of manager must be replaced with something else. This necessitates a level of curricular understanding and involvement in the learning process that is not evident in most schools. Effective schools research clamors for a proactive leadership posture but provides little guidance in actualizing that approach. The effective schools movement provides part of the answer for reforming schools. However, it too often focuses on diverse components more than the process or the end product. The result is that too many utilize the effective school correlates as nothing more than a technical recipe. This view, which borders on scientific management for some schools, simply fails to recognize education's diversity. Obviously, there remains a need for a different kind of leader in order to create an effective school.

Leadership Forces Hierarchy

Sergiovanni (1984, 1987) has developed a model which identifies five leadership forces as necessary for the creation of schools where excellence and effectiveness is the norm. He describes a force as "the strength or energy brought to bear on a situation to start or stop motion or change. Leadership forces can . . . bring about or preserve changes needed to improve schooling" (1984, p. 6).

The five forces are predicated on the concept that these forces can be used to improve or restructure schools. Each of the forces may exist at the classroom, building, or district level. This, in effect, means both teachers and administrators have the potential to impact the school for the better through their leadership. Briefly stated, the five forces as identified in Figure 2 are:

> Technical—derived from sound management techniques
>
> Human—derived from harnessing available social and interpersonal resources.
>
> Educational—derived from expert knowledge about matters of education and schooling
>
> Symbolic—derived from focusing the attention of others on matters of importance to the school
>
> Cultural—derived from building a unique school culture (Sergiovanni, 1984, p. 6).

Technical and human leadership have been the primary focus of research and administrator training for several years.

A closer look at the five forces provides some interesting possibilities as indicated in Table III. Technical leadership is essentially concerned with management or "the role of management engineer emphasizing such concepts as planning and time management, contingency leadership theories, and organizational structures" (Sergiovanni, 1987, p. 33). A

Figure 2. The Leadership Forces Hierarchy.

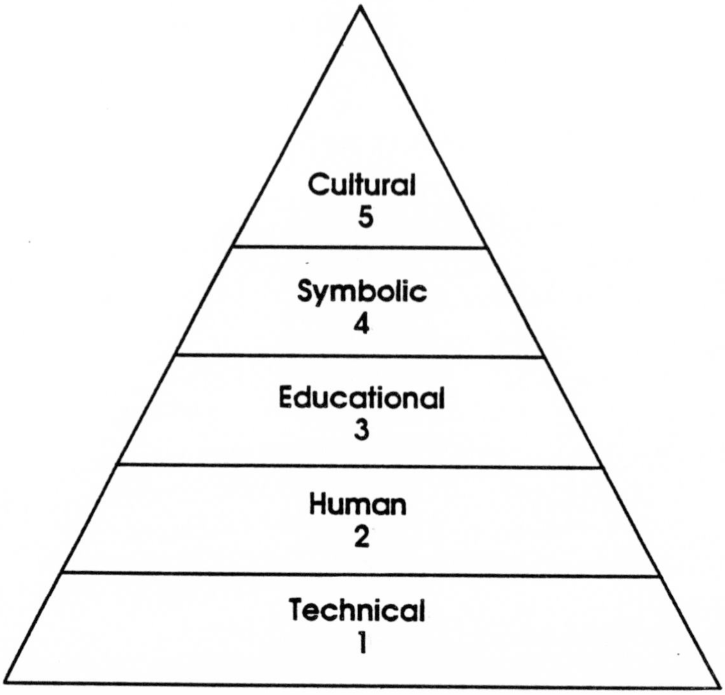
Cultural
5
Symbolic
4
Educational
3
Human
2
Technical
1

Sergiovanni, T. (1984). "Leadership and Excellence in Schooling." Educational Leadership, 41, 5: 4-13. Reprinted with permission of the Association for Supervision and Curriculum Development.

technical leader is a good planner, organizer, and coordinator. Technical leaders manage well and this insures that the school will function properly in regards to its daily activities. Systems management by good technical leaders is often seen as the most important role by boards of education and communities. Truthfully, too many administrators view this as not only their primary task but their only one.

Human leadership emphasizes human relations, motivation of subordinates, and interpersonal expertise. A human leader is also a human engineer. Human leaders improve morale, develop loyalty in subordinates, provide support, and improve others' skills. Most schools have administrators who are human leaders because without it "schooling problems are likely to follow" (Sergiovanni, 1987, p. 53).

Educational leaders bring "expert professional knowledge and bearing as they relate to teaching effectiveness, educational program development, and clinical supervision" (Sergiovanni, 1984, p. 6). Educational leaders are clinical practitioners who exhibit skills in counseling students and teachers, supervision, staff development, curriculum design, and diagnosing organizational as well as educational problems. Sergiovanni holds that these skills at one time were the core of administration training when principals were viewed as principal teachers or lead teachers. Works by Goodlad (1983) and Boyer (1983) and researchers of the effective schools movement have also emphasized a need for administrators to be educational leaders.

The first three forces of leadership—technical, human, and educational—are viewed by Sergiovanni (1983) as representative of those necessary "for competent schooling" (p. 7). Although these three may be important for the development of quality schools, they do not alone equate to excellence. Instead, symbolic and cultural leadership are forces needed to accomplish that goal. Symbolic leaders emphasize and express what is important to schools. In the role of chief, these leaders provide purpose and direction for schools by addressing "sentiments, expectations, commitments, and faith itself" (Sergiovanni, 1987, p. 56). Sergiovanni also believes that symbolic leaders are able to express their vision through words, symbols, and examples. Symbolic leaders assist people in rising above the daily managerial and structural activities and recognize the importance and significance of what the schools truly value.

The final leadership force is cultural. A cultural leader assumes the role of high priest. Cultural leaders articulate school missions and purpose by defining, identifying, and supporting the values and beliefs of the school. The cultural leader brings together the disparate elements of teachers, students, and staff into a team that is focused on the same mission or vision. This action provides school personnel, the community, and students with a new sense of belonging and personal significance. Cultural leaders understand that "cultural life in the schools is a constructed reality and school principals can play a key role in building this reality" (Sergiovanni, 1987, p. 59). This constructed reality or culture consists of norms, a shared past, common expectations, meanings, and a drive towards a future. Symbolic and cultural leaders influence the behavior, thought, and actions of those in a school. Without them, schools can never achieve a vision of a better future.

Sergiovanni's Forces of Leadership represents a powerful model that provides the reform movement with a better understanding of what has

Table III

THE FORCES OF LEADERSHIP AND EXCELLENCE IN SCHOOLING

Force	Leadership Role Metaphor	Theoretical Constructs	Examples	Reactions	Link to Excellence
1. Technical	"Management engineer"	• Planning and time management technologies • Contingency leadership theories • Organizational structure	• Plan, organize coordinate, and schedule • Manipulate strategies and situations to ensure optimum effectiveness	People are managed as objects of a mechanical system. They react to efficient management with indifference but have a low tolerance for inefficient management.	Presence is important to achieve and maintain routine school competence but not sufficient to achieve excellence. Absence results in school ineffectiveness and poor morale.
2. Human	"Human engineer"	• Human relation supervision • "Linking" motivation theories • Interpersonal competence • Conflict management • Group cohesiveness	• Provide needed support • Encourage growth and creativity • Build and maintain morale • Use participatory decision making	People achieve high satisfaction of their interpersonal needs. They like the leader and the school and respond with positive interpersonal behavior. A pleasant atmosphere exists that facilitates the work of the school.	
3. Educational	"Clinical practitioner"	• Professional knowledge and bearing • Teaching effectiveness • Educational program design • Clinical supervision	• Diagnose educational problems • Counsel teachers • Provide supervision and evaluation • Provide inservice • Develop curriculum	People respond positively to the strong expert power of the leader and are motivated to work. They appreciate the assistance and concern provided.	Presence is essential to routine competence. Strongly linked to, but still not sufficient for, excellence in schooling. Absence results in ineffectiveness.

4. Symbolic	"Chief"	• Selective attention • Purposing • Modeling	• Tour the school • Visit classrooms • Know students • Preside over ceremonies and rituals • Provide a unified vision	People learn what is of value to the leader and school, have a sense of order and direction and enjoy sharing that sense with others. They respond with increased motivation and commitment.	Presence is essential to excellence in schooling though absence does not appear to negatively impact routine competence.
5. Cultural	"High priest"	• Climate, clan, culture • Tightly structured values —loosely structured system • Ideology • "Bonding" motivation theory	• Articulate school purpose and mission • Socialize new members • Tell stories and maintain reinforcing myths • Explain SOPs • Define uniqueness • Develop and display a reinforcing symbol system • Reward those who reflect the culture	People become believers in the school as an ideological system. They are members of a strong culture that provides them with a sense of personal importance and significance and work meaningfulness which is highly motivating.	

happened in schools. Leaders have been educated and trained to be technical and human leaders, and occasionally educational ones. The need for preparing administrators to be symbolic and cultural leaders is real. Without a vision and without a process to imbue others with the sense of importance of that vision; and without a procedure to begin to actualize that vision, then any school improvement process will ultimately fail. Sergiovanni's model provides an important part of the puzzle in the search for quality schools.

CONCLUSION

This chapter had a three fold purpose. It was designed to (1) provide an overview of leadership definitions and recognize the absence of uniformity in those definitions; (2) review the historical development of administrative theory; and (3) briefly re-examine various leadership concepts, approaches, and theories often associated with leadership training and preparation. Finally, with the discussion of the effective school movement and various forces of leadership, it attempted to amplify the need for school administrators to select and utilize new modes of leadership.

Although the historical context of administrative theories and strategies is important, it is time to move past them. It is imperative that if this reform effort, or any improvement effort, is to succeed we must begin to view schools, the educational process, and the roles of the principal, the superintendent, and the staff in a new way. Sergiovanni (1987) is right when he indicates that training and research have primarily focused on technological and human leadership skills. Even the occasional attempt to prepare administrators to be educational leaders as per his model has been woefully inadequate.

The time has arrived to look at the purpose of schools and the methodology by which that purpose can be achieved. If what we have been doing isn't working, then it is time to seek a new method of doing things. That new approach may be restructuring or redesigning or reforming. The type of method doesn't matter but what does is the necessity to possess a vision of what it is we wish to accomplish before we do anything. The improvement process has always been the same; do it without really understanding what the ultimate result was to be. The educational community must possess a vision that reflects local needs and values. Every school is different and any attempt at imposing one single vision on all schools is doomed to failure. All schools are not, and cannot ever be, identical. An attempt to create a sameness in education is part of the problem, not part of the solution.

The real problem education often faces is the incessant desire to leap on the newest bandwagon, regardless of where that ideological wagon is heading or what the trip entails. Sadly, this has been the nature of most prior reform attempts and movements. Even the current one, especially during the first wave of policy mandates, developed a uniformity of approach that simply was unrealistic. Before there can be any improvement or reform, a local school or district must possess an organizational vision of what is to be accomplished. The development, and subsequent actualization, of that vision requires leaders in schools to be much more than human engineers and technicians. Then, and only then, will empowerment or restructuring or redesigning bring long-term improvement in the educational process. It's time to move into the future for both schools and their leaders. This can only be accomplished with a viable educational vision.

Chapter III

THE VISION CONCEPT

The reform movement and attempts at improving education have given cause to view the very structure of schools and the manner by which administrative theory and the preparation of school administrators has evolved. One item that stands out in this process is the powerful relationship between the degree of effectiveness of school administrators and any school improvement. Leadership studies have long focused on the ability of an administrator to accomplish tasks and achieve established organizational goals (Fiedler, 1967; House, 1971; Lipham, 1981; Reddin, 1970; Vroom & Yetten, 1973).

Recently, the leadership literature has introduced a much broader and more encompassing concept; that is the notion of vision (Guthrie & Reed, 1986; Roueche & Baker III, 1986; Stallings & Mohlman, 1981). Visionary leadership has emerged as a prominent characteristic of high performing administrators (Blumberg & Greenfield, 1980; Guthrie & Reed, 1986). The U.S. Department of Education publication, *Principal Selection Guide* (1987), stated that "effective school leaders have broad visions that are clear, active, ambitious, and performance oriented" (p. 5). It further indicated that effective administrators "create conditions to help them realize the vision" (p. 6).

As important as vision is to the effectiveness of a leader, as a construct it is elusive. There is no single definition, no item analysis, no magic formula, and no one book that has recounted how vision is formed, activated, or sustained. However, vision is clearly the force, the dream, towards which effective administrators continually strive in the shaping of their school district, individual site, or organization (Blumberg & Greenfield, 1980; Kouzes & Posner, 1987; Manasse, 1985; Rutherford, 1985; Shieve & Shoenheit, 1987). Administrators confronted by a multitude of tasks, economic restrictions, reform mandates, and increased community concerns must have a strong vision if schools are to achieve success. Vision provides the power and impetus for schools to do so.

This chapter will focus on two broad aspects. The first relates to the need for vision. This will be established by viewing the bureaucratic structure of schools that often hampers change and any improvement process. The need for vision will also be supported by contemplating the changing nature of society and ascertaining what possibilities may exist in the future. Given an educational structure that too often exists to maintain the status quo and a society that will confront a future totally dissimilar to its past, the need for an educational vision becomes quite apparent. The second component of this chapter will determine the meaning of vision by reviewing various relevant definitions and studies. A workable definition of vision will be established which will be utilized throughout the remainder of the book.

THE NEED FOR VISION

The reform process with its inevitable political mandates has attempted to improve the level of education provided to young people throughout the country. This process too often has resulted in reform for reform's sake without any viable idea as to what the future of education should hold. The result is that reform often reflects the need for institutions and leaders to do something without establishing a clear organizational destination. Change such as this is too often doomed to failure. That failure results because policy makers at the state and national level seldom understand the organizational complexity of the local school. Without a clear focus on what the local school should be, there is no vision. The reasons for an absence of an educational vision are closely tied to the structure of schools as well as to the rapidity of changes in today's society.

Bureaucratic Nature of Schools

Schools have functioned, but not always successfully, for the past one hundred years under the precept of the bureaucratic model. This well entrenched industrial or mechanistic model provides a system that effectively regulates teachers, students, and administrators (Bacharach & Conley, 1986). This means that rules, a system which coerced compliance, an explicitly defined organizational structure, and the specialization of tasks and behaviors became the norm. Many administrators, schooled in the pragmatic theories of top down administration, traditionally choose to utilize an authoritative, often dictatorial style of leadership (Barth,

1987). Control and order in such a system becomes more important than theoretical concepts such as creativity and flexibility. The maintenance of a tightly coupled organization with its emphasis on rules was the method selected by many administrators as a result of their training (Weick, 1982).

Given the current nature of teacher militancy and demands for an active involvement in the daily functioning of the school, as well as an increased clamor by the public for accountability, it is obvious that traditional administrative patterns will no longer be either adequate or acceptable. Administrators must be challenged to move from the authoritarian, managerial mode of operation to one best represented by proactive empowerment. This movement towards a new approach does not mean that all aspects of the bureaucratic structure should be jettisoned. Indeed, those components that coordinate and enhance the organization should remain but be carefully monitored as to their effectiveness. Any abuses and excesses in the bureaucratic model should be eliminated. Sergiovanni (1987) is correct when he indicates that successful administrators utilize such principles as empowerment, cooperation, and shared responsibility.

Schools must have a shared vision in order to improve. They will not be successful under the present structure where there is among teachers "a sense of discontent and malaise . . . a low sense of trust. . . . a sense of frustration at the 'nonteaching' demands. . . . " (Barth, 1990, p. 12). The adversarial relationship that has existed, partly because of the bureaucratic model, must cease. Teachers, administrators, parents, and students must work together to ascertain the vision for their school. Then, and only then, will reform succeed because it will be reform guided by an educational vision. A vision must exist if schools are to effectively prepare children for the 21st century. Demographic, cultural, technological, economic, social, and political changes will impact schools as never before. A well formulated educational vision can prepare schools and students to function effectively in the future.

Changing Structure of Society

Society as it is known today will not be the society of the future. So why should schools today be the same as schools of the future? It sounds logical that schools will change in response to societal changes and needs. Yet, even though the typical student of today is different from the student of twenty years ago, schools as organizations, except for minor differences, have remained essentially the same. This simply cannot continue into the 21st century. Schools and administrators must recognize and acknowledge the need for change and develop the vision to do so.

In the fall of 1988, there was a great deal of fanfare as the graduating class of the year 2000 began first grade. Yet, these children, as well as other children of this past decade, share some common characteristics that provide a preview of the future. These are:

1 out of 4 were from families who live in poverty;

14 percent were children of teenage mothers;

15 percent were physically or mentally handicapped;

14 percent were children of unmarried parents;

as many as 15 percent were immigrants who speak a language other than English;

40 percent will live in a broken home before they reach 18;

10 percent had poorly educated, often illiterate parents;

more than 25 percent were latch key children with no parent at home to greet them when they came home from school; and,

a quarter or more of them will not finish school (Johnson, 1988, p. 20).

These figures represent only a portion of the demographics that should be utilized in developing a vision for a school. Gary Marx, the assistant executive director of the American Association of School Administrators provided a set of startling figures at the AASA National Convention in Orlando, Florida, in 1989. They were:

Within the next thirty minutes:

41 students will lose one or both parents through divorce, separation, or death;

34 students will be added to the poverty rolls;

60 students will drop out of school;

29 students will run away from home;

14 students will give birth out of wedlock;

7 students will give birth out of wedlock for the second time;

228 students will be abused; and

641 students will do drugs (Marx, 1989).

These two sets of figures, and other similar statistics, should provide cause for thought as to how well schools are adjusting to the changing nature of society.

There are other indicators of the future that schools should be cognizant of in order to provide an appropriate education for all children. The population in the country has increased 59 percent between 1950 and 1986, increasing from 152 million to 241 million. In 1980, 20.3 percent of the population was between the ages of 14 and 24. By 1986, this number had declined to 18 percent and will continue to do so with some minor exceptions. By 1985, 54 percent of children who lived in female-headed families lived below the poverty level. In 1985, 4,772 young people were murdered and 5,121 committed suicide. Surprisingly, only 2,142 young people died of cancer in the same year. Also in 1985, 235,600 youth were arrested for drug abuse, larceny and theft, and drunk driving. Throughout the country, more than one in six arrests were of children under the age of eighteen (Office of Educational Research and Improvement, 1988).

Specific figures in education also paint an interesting picture. There was a continual increase in expenditures for schools between 1955 and 1986 with the average per pupil expenditure rising from $1571 to $4206. At the same time, the pupil/teacher ratio declined from 26.9 to 1 to 17.8 to 1. The percentage of dropouts declined between 1970 to 1986 from 15 percent to 12.6 percent. However, Scholastic Aptitude Test scores dropped from 479 to 424 on the verbal portion of the test. There was a momentary improvement in scores in 1983–84 as a result of early reform efforts (Office of Educational Research and Improvement, 1988).

The National Center for Education Statistics (NCES) in the report *The Condition of Education* (1990) indicated that although the dropout rate for black students had declined between 1975 and 1987, the proportion of black students below grade level had increased throughout the 1980s. Even with this, the graduation rate for blacks had increased from 59 to 83 percent. The NCES report also determined that only 51 percent of high school seniors in 1989 had used drugs compared to 66 percent in 1981. Even with this decline, the general public still perceives drug abuse as the major critical issue in schools. Teachers, on the other hand, indicate the most critical issue is the absence of parental concern and involvement in various educational issues (NCES, 1990).

The Condition of Education (1990) also reported several statistics that should be applauded. In 1987, women high school graduates were completing college at approximately the same rate as men. Chosen areas of study were still significantly different with only 20 percent of the degrees awarded in computer science or engineering going to women. Many women continued to select education as their field of endeavor. By 1987, blacks, Hispanics, and whites were generally selecting similar areas of study with the sciences, engineering, and business being chosen over education. The earning power of a college degree continued to increase. Men with college degrees earned 43 percent more than men with only high school diplomas. Women with college degrees, however, earned 68 percent more than female high school graduates. Generally, women still earned less than men in similar jobs (NCES, 1990).

Schools and educators need to be concerned about more than just demographics. Schools are closely tied to society and reflect the strengths and weakness exhibited by society. Therefore, school administrators need to be cognizant of future societal trends so that an appropriate response can be formulated. The United Way Strategic Institute (1990) recently identified nine forces that are impacting America as it moves into the 21st century. These forces include an aging American population, an increasingly diverse ethnicity, a redefinition of individual and societal roles, a global economic restructuring, and a redefinition of family and home life. The report identified certain areas of concern that will exist by the year 2000. Several of these are:

1. By the year 2000, the number of Americans in the 35–54 age group will increase 28 percent.
2. Hispanics and Asians will represent the greatest population increase, 56 percent and 76 percent respectively.
3. Alternative educational options such as magnet schools or year-round schools will continue to increase.
4. Businesses will become actively involved in social issues such as AIDS, illiteracy, and the educational curriculum.
5. Approximately 65 percent of all large corporations will provide remedial education programs for their employees.
6. Technology will play an increasing role in the daily lives of people.
7. Foreign investment in the United States will continue at a record pace.
8. There will be an emergence of new political and economic organizations throughout the world which will significantly impact the educational and economic system of this country.

9. Health care costs will triple by the year 2000.
10. The general health and well being of all the world's people will be significantly impacted by climatic changes.
11. The service sector will see massive growth while manufacturing will experience a general reduction in employees.
12. Consumer markets and economic bases will change as the population continues the shift to the West and South.
13. Nonfamily households headed by men will experience an increase of 72 percent by the year 2000. Single parent families headed by men will increase 42 percent, headed by women 31 percent.
14. Violent activities committed by the young will continue to grow as the national poverty rate, the number of homeless, and racial tensions increase.
15. The public infrastructure will continue to deteriorate at an alarming pace (United Way Strategic Institute, 1990, p. 9–16).

The Sixth General Assembly of the World Future Society also addressed future concerns by discussing six changing spheres such as the biosphere, sociosphere, technosphere, and politisphere (Wagner & Fields, 1989). Participants at this assembly were diverse and ranged from political leaders to sociologists to cosmonauts. The picture of the future envisioned by this group was similar to that of the United Way Strategic Institute. This assemblage of experts agreed that the biosphere was in trouble due to continued devastation of resources and atmospheric pollution. Environmental distress would eventually impact societal relationships, education, and the general economy of the world according to this group.

The Assembly discussed the changing nature of ethnicity in the United States and indicated that there would be a substantial increase in Hispanics and Asians. The nation's reliance upon technology would also escalate into the next century. A heightened interest in human rights would result because of expanded technological intrusions into each individual's life. There would be a refocusing on the issue of ethics in politics, business, and education because of societal changes.

In general, education was viewed as a system that has failed to deliver appropriately to all children. The result would be that many businesses would assume a portion of the educational process as the need to train undereducated and uneducated workers became more evident. The educational system of this country was "characterized by memorization and repetition, departmentalized learning, competitive efforts, isolated teaching environments, and cultural uniformity" (Wagner & Fields, 1989, p. 32). The collective belief shared by this group of futurists was that education would need to change and evolve just as the nation changed and that it would fail to serve the general populace if it did not do so. If education continued to provide services in the same manner, then others would supplant it as a viable institution (Wagner & Fields, 1989).

Much of what futurists view as probable has already begun to happen. The events in Europe with the reunification of Germany has created a new economic reality that the nation must respond to productively. The changing structure of families; increased minority participation in schools; burgeoning drug abuse; and, intensified youth violence have all impacted the educational institution. Technological advances have antiquated many of the traditional delivery systems utilized by schools. The computer and fiber optic lines have changed the very structure of much of American society. Yet, many schools instead of recognizing and responding to societal and technological changes continue the bureaucratic model with its compartmentalized tasks. Schools must respond energetically and creatively to the future.

If schools do not respond appropriately to the future then the alternatives are equally abhorrent. One option is to attempt to maintain the status quo and serve as a bastion for the past. The second equally unacceptable alternative is to leap on any new bandwagon that promises a new direction and identity. Either of these two can be equally disastrous. One option attempts to maintain that which can no longer be maintained, the other to change for the sake of change. The true answer for schools is to develop a vision for what should be accomplished in light of the future with recognition of the present and past. Without a vision of where schools are going and for what purpose, the educational process is doomed to failure.

WHAT IS VISION?

The literature provides many definitions of vision. Some of these definitions are general while others are much more specific and often relate to only one specialized aspect. Manasse (1985) provided a workable generic definition by describing vision as "the development, transmission, and implementation of a desirable future" (p. 150). Batsis (1987) perceived vision as more comprehensive than goals and objectives, because it allows one to see how these fit into the broader structure of the organization. Shieve and Shoenheit (1987) indicated that "a vision is a blueprint of a desired state. It is an image of a preferred condition that we work to achieve in the future" (p. 94).

In an extensive study of eight highly effective principals, Blumberg and Greenfield (1980) found that those with vision attempt to create an environment where their personal values provide a firm foundation for the school. Manasse (1982) also found that personal values were important. She indicated that effective administrators have a vision of a school that is firmly established and entrenched in publicly articulated values. These values are openly explained and discussed within the educational community. Manasse (1985) in further discussing the importance of personal values stated "this personalized approach to leadership may, in fact, run counter to some of the programmatic efforts to create 'effective schools' based on a set list of characteristics . . . " (p. 152).

An exhaustive study of leadership behavior by a team of University of Texas researchers (Rutherford, 1985) found that effective administrators could discuss the vision of their school without hesitation and could easily identify both long-range and short-range goals. "Typical goals included finding ways to meet the learning needs of all students, helping teachers adjust to a changing school population, raising test scores in a specific content area . . . " (p. 32) or a variety of other activities. Interestingly, this study found that teachers in a school with a principal with a vision were well aware of the educational vision and could relate it to others. Ineffective principals without a vision when asked to describe their vision "usually responded with a long pause and then a nonspecific statement . . . " (p. 32). These less effective principals often volunteered to provide Rutherford with a mission statement or some other similar material that is usually provided to state departments of education or an accrediting agency.

Burbach (1987) felt visionary leaders are those who have the insight to "see the larger social patterns within which they must operate" (p. 1). Glines (1987) saw visionary principals as those who are risk takers and "dreamers of the dreams" (p. 92). Greenbaum and Gonzalez (1987) indicated that effective leaders have "clear visions of what they want their schools to become and are able to translate these visions into district goals and expectations for their schools . . . " (p. 204).

Norris and Achilles (1988) equated visionary leadership to intuitive leadership. They felt that visionary leaders exhibited certain traits and characteristics. These are identified in Table IV. Visionary leaders would be those who combined both logic and intuition in problem solving and decision making. This whole brain approach represents a leadership behavior that is nontraditional in its approach.

Table IV
SAMPLE DESCRIPTORS USED TO COMPARE THE
LOGICAL/ANALYTICAL AND INTUITIVE/METAPHORICAL
THINKING AND DECISION-MAKING PROCESSES

Traditional *Logical/Analytical*	*Visionary* *Intuitive/Metaphorical*
Sequential	Holistic
Obvious	Exploratory
Convergent	Divergent
Selective	Random
Status-quo	Visionary
Systematic	Interpretive
Secure	Risk-Taking
Rational	Analogic
Intensional	Extensional
Verbal	Non-Verbal

Norris, C. S. & Achilles, C. M. (1988). Intuitive Leadership: A new dimension for education leadership. Planning and Changing, 19, 108–117. Reprinted by permission.

A significant portion of the literature relating to vision is business-oriented. Tichy and Ulrich (1984) discussed the need for visionary leaders to be transformational so that established objectives can be achieved. Morris (1987), however, identified the relevant leadership style as situational but did admit that any particular visionary leadership style is often "difficult to define" (p. 53). Much of the business literature associates vision with guiding the organization to a better, more efficient future and thus achieving organizational goals (Barnes & Kinger, 1986, Block, 1987; Burns, 1978; Labich, 1988; Pascarella, 1986; Peters & Waterman, 1982; and Sashkin, 1984). Gilmore (1988) indicated that a vision "must be balanced with a brutally realistic understanding of what is possible within the constraints of the situation" (p. 171). He indicated that a vision should not be allowed to be so unrealistic that it becomes nothing but an intellectual fantasy.

Several of the best descriptions of vision were proffered by Hickman and Silva (1984), Kouzes and Posner (1981), and Leavitt (1987). Hickman and Silva (1984) described vision as a "journey from the known to the unknown. . . . creating the future from a montage of facts, hopes, dreams.

... and opportunities" (p. 151). Leaders, according to Kouzes and Posner (1987), "have visions of what might be, and they believe they can make it happen" (p. 1). Leavitt (1987) equated visionary leaders with pathfinders and indicated that a "pathfinder is less concerned with prestige or glory than with causing movement toward some larger purpose..." (p. 61). He further indicated that a vision "usually starts in a fumbling, groping way, reaching toward some shadowy dream that cannot easily be verbalized or defined" (p. 62). It is certainly true that "vision grabs" and is "compelling" (Bennis & Nanus, 1985, p. 28).

Sashkin (1988) ascertained that vision has three essential elements. The first relates to the personality of the leader as well as to his/her cognitive skills. The second element reflects the ability to develop an organizational vision. The third "is the leader's ability to articulate the vision" (p. 124). Sashkin also identified four skills needed by visionary leaders. They were the ability to express the vision; the capacity to explain the vision; the potential to extend the vision to other activities; and, the skill to expand the vision in a multitude of ways (p. 128–130). Sashkin (1988) also indicated that the primary goal of visionary leaders is "the transformation of organizational cultures" (p. 153).

In a recent synthesis of the literature relating to visionary leadership, Grady and LeSourd (1990) identified five dominant qualities of a leader with vision. They found that leaders with vision are guided and motivated by personal values and convictions. They also established that these leaders have an intense commitment to the achievement of goals which they have identified as important for the organization. Additionally, visionary leaders strive to develop a common sense of purpose and direction among all members of the organization. They also found that visionary leaders are organizational innovators. Finally, visionary leaders consistently project and attest to a future that represents something better.

In an additional study, LeSourd and Grady (1990) utilized an attitude measurement instrument and several open-ended questions to interview several principals in California and Nebraska. These principals were selected from the earlier study cited above as the highest scoring and with a more positive attitude towards visionary leadership. The five attributes identified in their comprehensive leadership literature review were utilized for the attitude instrument. The results as identified in Table V indicate that visionary principals exhibit certain common attitudes toward leadership. The principals' responses supported the recog-

Table V
ATTITUDE SURVEY ITEMS: VISION SCALE

Attribute: Highly motivated by personal beliefs

Principals' actions should be consistent with their own beliefs.
Principals are reflective thinkers as well as action-oriented.
Principals should maintain personal goals even if some school patrons complain.

Attribute: Committed to attaining personal goals

Principals are committed to attaining their personal goals for their school.
Principals should do what is needed to get the results that they want.
The values and beliefs of the principal are the major influence upon the work of the people in the school.
The principal's own beliefs should be prominent in the atmosphere of the school.
Principals must actively work to promote their ideals in the school.

Attribute: Value a prominent, shared school ideology

Teachers work hard when the principal makes school goals clear.
Principals should vigorously articulate school goals at every opportunity.
In good schools, the principal and teachers are committed to common purposes.
School climate is different in each school, because of the strong influence of each school staff's beliefs about students and learning.
Successful schools have a clearly understood philosophy.
Goals will be attained in a school in which everyone knows what is important for success.

Attribute: Predisposed toward innovation

Temporary disruption of school operations is sometimes necessary to achieve progress.
A good principal can be expected to take innovative actions.
The principal can be expected to take innovative actions.
The principal should create an atmosphere of creativity in the school.
Good principals are driven by a desire to create new ideas.
Principals must be willing to take risks.

Attribute: Visualize a better future

Leaders should be driven by their vision of a better future.
Some principals become well-known because they are heroic, visionary leaders.
Principals should spend time actively planning for the future.
Wise principals focus their school on an image of what the school should be in the future.
School principals should have a view of a future which is better than the present.

From High School Journal, Vol. 73, No. 2, December/January 1990. Published by the School of Education, University of North Carolina, Chapel Hill, © 1990 University of North Carolina Press. Reprinted by permission of the publisher.

nition and importance of personal values, ideology, goal attainment, innovation, and future orientation.

However one defines vision, it is clear from the literature that effective administrators possess it. Vision is highly personal, although it conceivably can be shaped by a "plural parentage" of teachers, parents, and students (Murphy, 1988, p. 656). Vision is a destination, albeit there may be many detours and roadblocks before the objective is achieved. Vision is essentially intangible. It cannot be touched, felt, or seen but it is essential that it exist. Vision is a sweet dream of the future regardless of organizational or environmental constraints. It provides a sense of direction. A visionary administrator in a school is not afraid of stating, "This is what I believe; this is what the school can accomplish; and this is where we are going to be in one year, five years, and ten years." Vision is a powerful force that guides, cajoles, directs, and facilitates accomplishment.

CONCLUSION

A crucial aspect of proactive leadership is the development of a vision that not only calls for excellence but establishes an educational environment and culture where this can be achieved. Administrators must be willing to ask the questions, "What are we doing, is it working for us, can it be done in a better way to accomplish our goals?" and then listen to the answers. Administrators who are leaders, and not simply managers, must be able to model and articulate their vision while consistently striving to actualize the organization they envision.

An administrator with vision is able to maintain a focus on that vision through any organizational turmoil or change. Rutherford (1985) found that teachers recognized the existence of an administrative vision and were able to describe the vision albeit often in different terms. He found that teachers and students in a school with visionary leadership identified school as a good place. He also ascertained that visionary leaders provide meaningful direction to seemingly insignificant daily activities through their modeling. A vision unifies a school and increases the emotional support of those in the organization (Littley & Fried, 1988). All within such an organization work collegially to achieve the vision and believe their daily contributions are important in realizing the espoused vision (Manasse, 1985).

Vision is important because it serves as a guide for the school's administrators, faculty, students, and support staff. It helps establish the climate for the school, because expectations, goals, and purposes are clear and cogent. Vision attains results, and as it does teachers and students become aware of their accomplishments and experience a sense of pride in their involvement.

Chapter IV

DEVELOPING A PERSONAL VISION

A vision begins at a very personal level with an individual leader. If a personal vision does not exist and if effective leadership does not attempt to actualize the vision, then the result is often either organizational chaos as multiple goals are haphazardly pursued or organizational malaise as the maintenance of the status quo becomes the primary motive of the organization. The leader and his/her role in the development of a vision have been identified as crucial to organizational effectiveness (Bennis & Nanus, 1985; Block, 1987; Grady & Le Sourd, 1988; Kouzes & Posner, 1987; Manasse, 1982; Rutherford, 1985; Shieve & Shoenheit, 1987).

Bennis (1989) in his recent work, *Why Leaders Can't Lead*, discussed the need for leaders who are able to manage and control the bureaucratic inertia that exists in many organizations. This intransigence found in numerous organizations creates a type of "incestuous relationship . . . with middle management devoting its time to justifying its existence" (p. 145). Bennis observed that there is a critical paucity of leaders and that "people in authority must develop the vision and . . . call the shots" (p. 154). The necessity for a vision to exist in industry holds equally true for schools and public education.

The question remains as to how does one possess or develop a vision. Is a person born with certain genetic characteristics and traits that tend to lend themselves to visionary leadership? Does the environment in which one exists impact the ability to develop a vision and to actualize it? Is there one essential element in vision development? Is there a magic formula that can help one become a visionary leader? There are no simple answers to these questions. The degree to which traits, organizational environment, and the situation interact to impact vision development is not as important as the need for one to exist. Although all of the above are important elements in the process, the truth is that one must have a proclivity to become a visionary leader or a vision can not be effectively developed.

It is this author's contention that for those who possess the inclination

54

for developing a vision as well as a desire to do so, that certain procedures or steps can be followed that will assist in the development or clarification of a vision. The process described in this chapter will simply be an intellectual exercise for one who desires to be nothing more than a technical leader solving daily problems with little thought to the future of the organization. The vision development process will not be useful for the individual desirous of maintaining personal security within the organization at all costs. The procedure also will be of little use to the human leader who only desires to be liked and has difficulty in making tough decisions or dealing with stressful processes.

Figure 3. Steps in Developing Vision and Sustaining a Vision for a School.

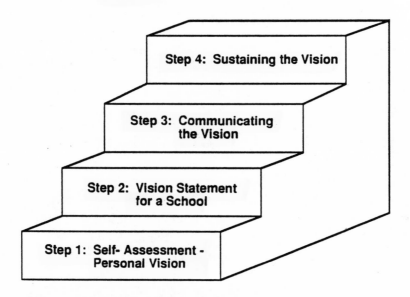

Becoming a leader with a vision and then bringing that vision to fruition is possible with the procedure discussed in this chapter and the remainder of the book. Figure 3 provides a schematic view of the total step process. The essential component in the whole procedure is that one must desire to be a proactive leader with a goal of creating an optimal functioning organization. If one wishes to be more than a manager and envisions himself/herself as an individual who can lead, then the process is relevant and useful. Traits, the environment, the organization, and the situation hold a degree of relevance in vision development, but the cardinal element is an intrinsic commitment to proactive leadership.

CLARIFYING/DEVELOPING A PERSONAL VISION

A personal vision essentially represents one's dream of what could be in an organization or school. A personal vision is uniquely owned by the individual who develops it and is not confined or constricted by organizational realities. It is a unique view of the future that directly reflects personal beliefs and values. The research has emphasized again and again that strong personal values are a key in the development of a well thought out personal vision (Bennis & Nanus, 1985; Manasse, 1982; Rutherford, 1985; Shieve & Shoenheit, 1987).

Since personal values hold such importance, it is useful to distinguish the difference between a value and a belief. Essentially values represent those items to which one holds fast, and they exemplify what is most important to each person. Values are most often developed early in life as a result of the interaction of family and society. Rarely does one change basic values without a moral conflict and intense struggle. Beliefs, on the other hand, change quite frequently as one grows and matures. Beliefs may often appear initially as values, yet beliefs are much more numerous and nebulous. A sense of family or the importance of an education represent values, while the purchase of certain items because they are viewed as being better or the support of certain faddish political concepts reflect beliefs.

Recognition of one's values is important in developing a personal vision because the vision directly reflects the values of the person who develops it. Figure 4 provides an overview of the components that interact in the development of a personal vision. As these various components interact, it is important that one begins to think about the vision in terms that avoid organizational or educational jargonese. Every profession or occupation develops unique ways to communicate. This is often accomplished by utilizing acronyms or catch phrases. A personal vision is best when it reflects less jargon and more of the leader's values as he/she develops it.

Developing or clarifying a personal vision is easier to effect when done sequentially by first determining personal values and building from there. It is also easier to accomplish, given the nature of the process, by referring to the reader in a personal manner. The word "you" will be utilized in order to personalize this process. A good starting point is to spend some time to ascertain those attributes that represent a successful leader and those that exemplify one not quite so successful. A

Figure 4. Considerations in Developing a Personal Vision.

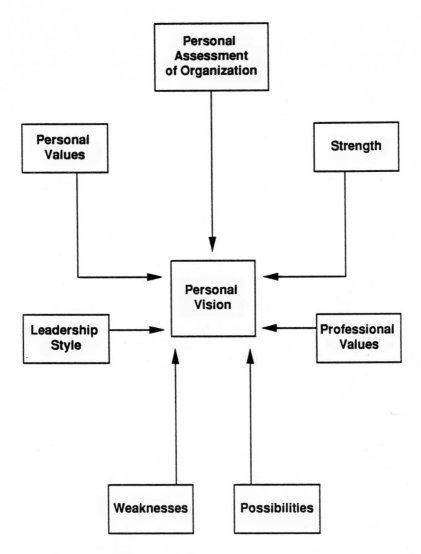

simple listing of characteristics, five or six, in each of the areas is sufficient. Once these are listed, then you should reflect on the identified attributes and how they relate to or represent your skills and abilities. This is a first step in analyzing your aptitude and abilities. Do the identified characteristics of the successful leader epitomize your personal characteristics? Or, are they best represented by the identified characteristics and attributes of a less effective leader?

The next step is even more personal and essentially represents how you hope others perceive you as a leader. It may appear to be a bit macabre but it is useful. Write your own epitaph. That is, write it in a manner as you would hope those in your school or organization would write it. The epitaph should be no more than fifteen words. The idea behind this is that it allows you to really respond in the way you would hope others would. The epitaph helps you to determine what is important to you because it looks at values. The epitaph will be utilized in the writing of the personal vision.

Everyone continually establishes personal and professional goals throughout his/her life. It is important to evaluate what has been accomplished throughout your career. Drawing an individual professional lifeline can assist in recognizing past accomplishments as well as assist in determining future goals. The lifeline is a way to graphically illustrate the various peaks, valleys, and plateaus of a career. Begin the lifeline at the left edge of a sheet of paper and label this area the past. The center of the sheet represents the present and the right side should reflect what you hope to accomplish in the immediate future of three to five years. As the professional lifeline is drawn, label any significant events that have taken place either in the past or most recently in the present. On the far right side, the future, dream a little and identify professional goals in the three to five year range. Be as complete as possible in the lifeline. This may take some time but the type of items identified and plotted directly reflect personal values. Figure 5 provides an example of a completed lifeline.

There are certain questions that can assist in evaluating the professional lifeline. How well does the lifeline reflect the reality of your career? Does the lifeline indicate any of the previously identified leadership attributes and characteristics of effective leaders? The last question is the most relevant one. Given identified successes or setbacks, can you determine any professional growth that came from any of the experiences labeled in the lifeline? The professional lifeline provides an opportunity for a person to identify those matters which have meant the most and have impacted to the greatest degree.

The next step represents a series of self-evaluation and value recognitions questions. Effective leaders clearly recognize their strengths and weaknesses. They also are able to readily discuss important values and beliefs. The intent of the following self-evaluation questions is to provide an opportunity for an examination of your values and abilities. The

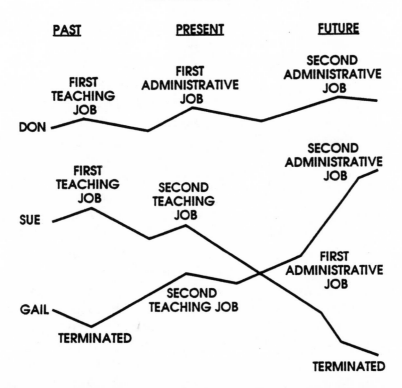

Figure 5. Develop a Professional Lifeline.
List Successes/Failures.

first aspect is to identify any leadership strengths that you may possess. What are you good at? Identify as many as possible but you should be able to attest to at least five or six strengths. Secondly, designate five or six leadership-oriented weaknesses. Sometimes perceived items can be both a strength and a weakness. For instance, organization as a strength is a useful attribute, but as a weakness it can indicate that task completion takes precedence over other things or that one finds it difficult to effectively delegate.

The third question asks you to select those things that are most valued in your professional career. The answers can be either very concrete or extremely abstract. For example, power may represent an abstract concept unless it means the power to hire and fire others. That makes it much more concrete. The last question in this area is designed to reflect to some extent the future components of the professional lifeline. What are three things that you as a leader wish to accomplish in your school or organization within the next three to five years? Compare your answers to the professional lifeline. The professional lifeline often will reflect highly personal career goals while the answer to this specific question represents organizational goals. However, interestingly the organizational goals for the next three to five years often are an elaboration of the personal goals and values established with the lifeline.

Good leaders understand and recognize their abilities. Looking at one's strengths and weaknesses is a good beginning to this process. Effective leaders also can readily identify factors which motivate them to achieve. The following questions are designed to assist in ascertaining what personally motivates you. First, with what style of leadership are you most comfortable and why do you choose to utilize this leadership approach? Answer this question in any manner but try to avoid an extensive theoretical textbook answer. The next question is very important. Why did you choose to become an administrator? What do you *really* want to prove, to accomplish, to achieve as a school administrator? The answer given will directly reflect personal values. The third question focuses on how you perceive the significance of the job as an administrator. What are some things that make the job worthwhile and important? Identify as many elements as possible that make the job a good one. The final question again is designed to determine personal values and is closely tied to the epitaph you previously wrote. How would you like to be remembered as an administrator by the teachers, the students, and the community? Compare the epitaph with the answer you just supplied. Is there a significant variance between the two answers? If there is then analyze the answers. One answer may reflect values, the other beliefs. Table VI provides a summary of all of the questions to this point and can be useful in viewing the whole process.

At this point, carefully evaluate all of your answers. Look at the epitaph, the professional lifeline, your strengths and weaknesses, your predominant leadership style, the important things you wish to accomplish, and the reasons given for becoming an administrator. One last test is to determine whether the answers truly represent what *you* value and believe or only reflect what you assume society would want you to believe and value. It may be necessary to change some of the answers. However, only the person answering the questions will truly know the overall validity of the answers.

Once all of this is accomplished, it is time to begin writing a personal vision statement. This vision statement represents what you wish to see accomplished. It should not be hampered or restricted by the realities of

Table VI
SUMMARY OF QUESTIONS IN DEVELOPING A PERSONAL VISION

What are my five greatest strengths?

What are my five greatest weaknesses?

What are three things I most value in my professional life?

With what style of leadership am I most comfortable?

What are the most important things I want to accomplish in this school/school district?

What do I want to prove as an administrator?

How would I like to be remembered as an administrator?

any organizational, economic, social, or political restraints. It should manifest what you wish to accomplish as a leader. In effect it represents what your school should be in an idealistic sense. Vision statements often reflect universal or global values such as equity and justice (Shieve & Schoenhert, 1987), but they may also represent more personal values and concerns. A vision statement should not be long. This author believes it should be no more than twenty-five words in length. The shorter and more concise it is, the more it represents a personal vision devoid of extensive jargon.

After writing the personal vision statement, take a moment and evaluate it. Does it say what you want it to say? Does it reflect your personal and professional values? Do you believe the statement and support it? Are you willing to strive to bring the vision to a reality? If the answer is yes to all of the questions, then the personal vision is viable. The development of a personal vision holds two purposes. First, it represents the values of the school's leader. Secondly, it provides a goal for the leader to strive towards. However, a personal vision is just that—personal. It does not always reflect the organization, i.e., school, and its culture or its strengths and weaknesses. The subsequent creation of a viable organizational vision by the leader allows for the melding of the highly personal, individually owned vision into an overall personal organizational vision. This then provides a more reasonable destination for the vision process as it eventually evolves to include others.

DEVELOPING A PERSONAL ORGANIZATIONAL VISION

The second major aspect of the development of a vision is the creation of a personal organizational vision. The organizational vision represents what a leader wishes to see the school or organization accomplish and often reflects the values exhibited in the personal vision. The development of a personal organizational vision is accomplished in much the same manner as the formulation of a personal vision. The process begins with a recognition of the attributes of an effective school, focuses specifically on the target school, and concludes with the development of a personal organizational vision for that school. After the personal vision has been conceptualized and the personal organizational vision has been developed, others will then become involved in generating an overall organizational vision for the school.

As the process of developing a highly personalized organizational vision begins, it is useful to generate a list of characteristics and attributes of a highly effective school. This is best completed by utilizing one's experience but can be complemented by researching the concept of school effectiveness. Either way, the creation of a list of attributes and characteristics provides one with something to measure the local, target school against. The converse of this is to identify any characteristics or attributes that exist in a weak, ineffective school. Once both lists are generated, it is useful to compare the various characteristics to the local school for which the personal organizational vision is being developed. It is also advantageous to identify any relatively poor characteristics or attributes that may be converted to strengths through the utilization of effective leadership strategies. Figure 6 provides an overview of the process for developing a personal organizational vision.

This first step is designed to assist you in thinking about schoolwide strengths and weaknesses. A second step puts the focus on the local school or organization. Basic knowledge about the school is crucial in the development of a personal organizational vision. At this point, identify five to seven strengths of your local school. What are the things it does well? What are the best components of the school? Also identify five to seven weaknesses relating to the school. What are areas that need immediate improvement? What are the weakest elements in the school? The best or poorest aspects of a school may represent people, the curriculum, or facilities.

Once these are listed, then determine whether or not others within the

Figure 6. Considerations in Developing a Vision for a School.

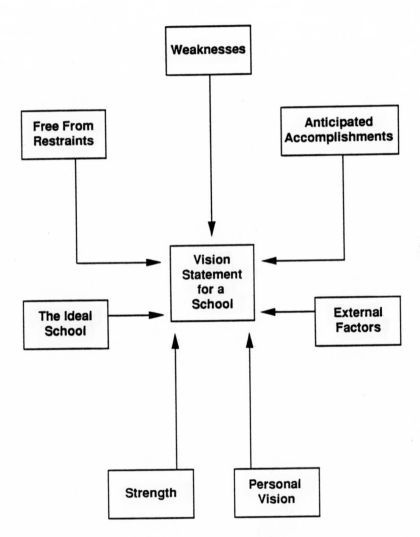

school would agree with your assessment. Which groups or local organizations would agree or disagree with your assessment of strengths and weaknesses? If there is a tremendous difference between your assessment of the school and that of others, how will this difference be handled? If one is to be a leader, there must be followers to lead but if no one else perceives any problems, how can this be effectively addressed and resolved?

There are several other specific factors that need to be evaluated before an achievable personal organizational vision can be conceived. What are any "people" strengths in the school that can be capitalized on in the development of an overall organizational vision? What are the "people" weaknesses that can hamper the development and actualization of an organizational vision? Are there any concomitant factors external to the school that can be amplified in the development of an organizational vision? In many ways, this process is similar to Lewin's Force Field Analysis (1947) in that one needs to determine what forces or elements can be better utilized in achieving the vision and what forces need to be controlled or restrained that could hamper actualizing the vision. Table VII provides a summary of the questions used in the development of a personal organizational vision.

Table VII
SUMMARY OF QUESTIONS IN DEVELOPING
A PERSONAL ORGANIZATIONAL VISION

What are the strengths of this school?

What are its weaknesses?

What are various interpersonal strengths and weaknesses of this school?

How well do the various components of this organization function?

What does your ideal school look like?

After the above questions are fully answered, and the answers analyzed, it is then time to write the personal organizational vision statement. It is important to recognize that this still represents a personal view and does not necessarily reflect what may be adopted after the involvement of others. However, an administrator's personal vision and personal organizational vision statements based on personal values provide a foundation for all subsequent organizational vision development. The personal organizational vision statement should be short, again no longer than twenty-five words with a minimal amount of educationalese.

After the organizational vision statement is written, it should be evaluated in light of the same analysis questions as before. Does it say what you want it to say? Does it reflect your personal and professional values? Do you believe it and support it? Are you willing to bring the vision to a reality? Assuming the answers are in the affirmative, it is then useful to compare the two vision statements. One may be surprised at the degree of similarity between the two statements. This high degree of likeness is because they both reflect the individual values of the person writing them. If there are any striking areas of incongruence, it is important to ascertain why the areas exist and how as a leader you will resolve the dissimilitude.

It is also imperative that the separate vision statements be further judged in the light of the "real" world. Will the personal organizational vision statement give those within the school a purpose for being involved in achieving the vision? Does your exhibited behavior as an administrator reinforce and support the two vision statements? What are the overall strengths of the vision statements? What is it about them that makes the statements powerful and desirable? Does the personal organizational vision statement reflect or conflict with community values? If it is in conflict with community values, then to what degree are you willing to compromise your personal organizational vision? Will you attempt to determine strategies that will alter or change the culture of the community?

If a personal vision statement reflects one's values, then what happens if the values espoused in the vision are diametrically opposed to the values evident in the community? These are not necessarily philosophical questions. They are intended to assist in the resolution of a potential value conflict. Leaders of all types of organizations are often faced with similar dilemmas. If the vision is important and represents what you see as vital and necessary, then the choices and options are extremely limited. If one cannot get others to accept and support the vision, then you either change the vision, give it up completely, or go someplace where the vision will be accepted. If the vision represents only rhetoric, then the solution is easily resolved and one simply changes the vision or forgets it. If it is real, then the decision is obvious. Fight for it and possibly win, but if you lose be ready to go to a new organization. Visionary leaders understand the probabilities and are still willing to fight for their vision.

CONCLUSION

The development of a personal vision and a personal organizational vision is only the beginning of the vision process but it is the most important part of the process. Without a strong personal vision and personal organizational vision, the leader is not able to effectively impact the school because he/she doesn't know where it is going. Personal values directly influence the development of a personal vision. These same values, when combined with organizational realities, influence the creation of an organizational vision. Only after these two visions are developed can one begin to design an overall organizational vision through the involvement of other stakeholders.

The key to the whole process lies with the leader and whether he/she has a clear vision of what the school can and should become. Without a vision, the local school will continue to function, and even educate children, but will never reach its true potential. The vision process is a sequential system that begins with a personal assessment and moves to the development of a personal vision and a personal organizational vision. After the involvement of others, an overall vision statement for the school is developed. The organizational vision is then communicated in a variety of ways to all within and outside the school. A strategic plan with incremental goals and objectives is developed to begin to actualize the vision. The movement towards the vision must be constantly analyzed and adjusted as necessary. The vision remains fairly constant but the process evolves. A vision may never be achieved but the attempt to do so can bring innumerable achievements and a multitude of improvements.

Throughout the total vision development process, the administrator/ leader continues to guide, facilitate, cajole, and even occasionally manipulate those involved in the process. He/she must never lose sight of the personal vision and the personal organizational vision. The process succeeds on the basis of the quality of leadership provided by the school administrator. Too much leadership and the result is viewed as a product of autocratic dictatorial. Too little leadership and a laissez faire attitude may prevail with little or no directional movement. The result is vision fragmentation. Leadership that is properly manifested is the essential ingredient for success of the process. The leader's individual values serve as the guidepost for all other activities in vision development.

Chapter V

UNDERSTANDING GROUP DYNAMICS

A visionary leader understands and effectively utilizes group processes. He/she has an awareness of group development, group roles, and an ability to design groups so that their potential may be maximized. A leader also has the capability to successfully resolve group conflicts. Knowledge about group processes, and the ability to use that knowledge, is imperative in the development of an overall organizational vision.

The visionary leader must be able to infuse groups with an air of excitement and commitment as they begin the process of creating a comprehensive vision for the school. This capability to lead various groups must be accomplished by walking a thin line between autocrat and pure democrat. By understanding group developmental theory, the visionary leader can establish an appropriate group structure with reasonable parameters and guidelines that facilitate group interaction and production. When necessary, the visionary leader provides guidance and expertise in the vision building process by working with those who hamper the group and empowering those who support it. The visionary leader keeps group members focused on the task at hand by establishing realistic expectations and a reasonable group charge that clearly and explicitly guide the group.

The group is assisted by the leader to establish short-term and long-term goals that acceptably move the school towards actualizing the vision. The intent is to involve others in the vision building, communicating, and actualizing process so that the vision is widely supported by those both within and outside the school organization. Developing an overall organizational vision, with subsequent procedures to turn it into a reality, is not an easy process and certainly not a tidy one. It is imperative that the visionary leader not lose sight of his/her personal and professional vision of the organization. The leader's personal organizational vision serves as a guiding force within the total vision development process.

This chapter will address issues relating to group development, group roles, and group design that can ensure the success of the vision building process. Although the knowledge of group theories is helpful and necessary, the visionary leader's dedication to his/her vision is the essential element in the vision process.

GROUP DEVELOPMENTAL THEORIES

It is important to involve as many people as possible in the vision process. Those asked to participate should represent a wide range of stakeholders with various backgrounds, education, and even levels of support for the school. The diversity of group members can become an asset once consensus is reached on the overall vision and on the method by which it will be actualized. Taking the easy path of creating only a homogeneous group that accepts and supports everything the leader suggests, establishes an opportunity for those who were left out of the process to become active saboteurs and destroy what has been developed. It is far better to initially involve as diverse a population as possible because extensive diversity creates a foundation of community support. Certainly, a variegated group is more difficult to work with, but it is better to accept and recognize this from the inception so that the vision process has a greater opportunity for success.

The visionary leader will also find it necessary to decide how various groups will be utilized in developing an overall organizational vision. The larger the group the more aggregate is the knowledge, but it becomes harder to accomplish tasks and maintain the group's focus. It is best to initially have a large, heterogeneous group and break this group into smaller ones which eventually converge back into one large unified group. The ability to design successful groups becomes easier to accomplish once one accepts the concept that all groups evolve somewhat differently yet in a comparable manner. Groups develop in a sequential, predictable order over a period of time. It can even be helpful to think of groups as living organisms that evolve, change, and mature as a result of experiences, knowledge, and opportunities.

Any developmental process of groups must also be viewed in light of the sociological differences of each group member. Group members' sex, ethnicity, age, socioeconomic status, and educational background contributes to the success or failure of each group. Additional elements that may influence group development and group potential are personal and community aspirations; the nature of the school as an organization; the ruralness or urbanization of the community; and abilities of the visionary leader to work with a broad spectrum of people. It is also necessary to recognize that although the formal group structure may be quite specific, it is often the informal group structure that is often the more powerful of the two. The informal group, just as the formal one, will have its own norms, roles, and expectations.

Although there are a multitude of group developmental theories, for the purpose of this work it is not necessary to discuss every theory in detail. Only two of the major approaches to group development will be presented. Napier and Gershenfeld (1985) advanced one of the best views of group processes when they developed a composite theory representing various approaches. They identified a five-stage process through which all groups progress. The five stages were: (1) the beginning; (2) movement towards confrontation; (3) compromise and harmony; (4) reassessment; and (5) resolution and recycling (p. 459–466). The basic tenets of this composite theory advanced by Napier and Gershenfeld (1985) represented an important synthesis of various theories espoused by several leadership and group theorists.

The beginning represents the stage of group development where people tend to observe and gather as much information as possible about the group task and about other group members. Each group member comes to the group with certain life experiences and personal expectations that may impact their ability to function initially in the group. The beginning represents a time of inhibition for some members as well as a time of testing of group limits as norms and expectations are established and accepted by group members. This first stage of group development also represents a time when members are more security minded. This concern for security in the group guides each member into seeking to establish a role in which they will be comfortable. At this stage, it is essential that the group not be pushed too quickly or group members will never fully adjust to the group and its task.

The second stage, a movement toward confrontation, is a normal result of group members becoming more comfortable and beginning to seek to establish their individual spheres of influence. Gaining power and recognition becomes important to many at this stage. Group roles become more entrenched and members begin to develop alliances and garner support for their personal agendas. The result of this newly found need for power and assertiveness is the creation of an air of caution, suspicion, and mistrust which can cripple the ability of a group to effectively function. Ideas and issues often become polarized as each member tests his/her influence to the limit. Some members become frustrated with the power needs of others and either lash out or withdraw in anger or disappointment. A few may recognize the destructive bent of the group and by utilizing a variety of methods move the group to a third developmental stage. Some groups never move past the confrontation stage and continue to exist as a group but in actuality cease to function. The visionary leader recognizes the need to allow each group to find its own identity without destroying its effectiveness. However, the visionary leader is not afraid to step in when necessary to guide and assist a group so it may move forward. This requires a degree of skill and timing on the part of the visionary leader.

The third stage as identified by Napier and Gershenfeld (1985) represents compromise and harmony. This stage is generally arrived at as group members recognize that a failure to compromise will result in a collapse of the group. Movement to this stage is often accomplished by members who serve as intermediaries between polarized members. Some utilize humor in dealing with the hostility that has been generated in previous group stages. Some members develop new alliances and effectively block those who have become overtly hostile and unproductive. Whatever method is chosen, this third stage finds the easing of group dissension with a greater acceptance of either individual or group deviation. This acceptance of aberrant behavior lasts as long as the behavior does not impact the effectiveness of the group.

Group members actively collaborate with each other in this third stage. There is an overriding sense of caution as members overtly avoid any type of hostility. The group still seeks an open, honest atmosphere but couples this with concern for the whole group. The generation of new volatile issues are often avoided by group jokes and laughter. Because there still may be a degree of underlying tension between some members, the group may fail to address important issues. Harmony for the sake of harmony can paralyze the group and hamper its effectiveness. A visionary leader needs to be able to recognize this sense of group inertia, and even if it means some conflict, move the group into the next stage. This can be successfully accomplished by narrowing and restating the group charge as well as group parameters.

The fourth stage, reassessment, recognizes the group's establishment of new organizational and operational restrictions. If the organizational restraints are too tightly structured, overall problems of the group may continue to exist and even multiply. Certainly, group decisions may be more efficiently formed with the new limitations, but underlying group interpersonal problems often continue to exist. There is frequently a level of fear that group conflict will begin anew. If conflict can be avoided, the group generally begins to accept and support concepts such as individual accountability, shared responsibility, and a more formalized division of labor.

The final stage as advanced by Napier and Gershenfeld (1985) is called resolution and recycling. The group is fairly mature, having survived the first four stages, and has an ability to resolve group problems. The level of productivity in the final stage is quite high. There generally is a positive feeling among group members toward both the task and each other. This does not mean that a crisis cannot result in a degree of conflict. If conflict comes, the group is now better equipped to resolve it. The level of group maturity directly relates to how effective or ineffective the group will be in dealing with a conflict.

According to Napier and Gershenfeld (1985) all groups progress through similar stages of development. Tuckman and Jensen (1977) espoused a group developmental theory that is as relevant to the visionary leader as that discussed above. They, too, concluded that all groups progress through five stages of development that are comparable to those identified by Napier and Gershenfeld (1985).

Tuckman and Jensen's (1977) stages of group processes are forming, storming, norming, performing, and adjourning. All five of these stages should be viewed by looking at both task orientation and a concern for the advancement of interpersonal relationships. The first stage, forming, refers to the coming together of a new group and the sense of uneasiness that can result from a new situation. This initial period of apprehension and caution is followed by a period of storming. Storming represents a stretching of group boundaries as group members assert themselves in establishing their personal realm of influence and power. Conflict often results that can destroy the group if the next stage is not achieved.

The third stage is called norming. This is a time when group and individual norms are firmly established. These norms may be both implicit and explicit. The increased sense of order results in a greater focus on the task and leads to the fourth stage. Performing finds an intense focus by the group on the task. The group is well solidified in its membership, its roles, and group norms. Productivity is extremely high as a sense of camaraderie increases. The final stage, adjourning, comes about as the group nears the completion of its task and either prepares for new tasks or group dissolvement. Once the initial task is completed, groups need new challenges. If these are not forthcoming then the group's function is over and the group should disband. To remain together as a group but without purpose or function is both ineffective and inefficient. The visionary leader understands that a group is not formulated to last forever and knows when to terminate it.

Cohen and Smith (1976) espoused a totally different view of group development. They indicated that all groups develop around five themes. Each group must effectively address each theme if it is to function in an effective manner. The five themes are anxiety, power, norms, interpersonal relationships, and personal growth. One or more of the themes may be the focus of the group at various times but all five themes are usually present in various degrees. The major difference between the view of Cohen and Smith (1976) and others is that they believe the group themes may develop within the group at any time and in any order. Any theme which is not dealt with appropriately by the group may result in a loss of group productivity.

Whichever theory one accepts is not as important as the knowledge that groups are not static entities. A basic understanding of group development provides a leader with a sense of comprehension that is necessary if an organizational vision is to be developed. This knowledge of group processes remains important as the group eventually develops strategies which communicate the vision to others. A leader who does not understand group developmental processes will often become frustrated and resort to coercive behavior in order to accomplish the task. A high degree of coercion on the part of a leader inevitably results in group alienation, not commitment. A visionary leader understands this and uses his/her knowledge of group theories as the means by which the organization can better be served in the development of an overall organizational vision.

DESIGNING GROUP PARAMETERS

A visionary leader must be able to effectively utilize groups in order to develop a vision and a plan by which the vision can become a reality. This necessitates the possession of a well formulated personal and professional vision by the leader. He/she must also understand group development and how the various developmental stages of groups directly impacts the functioning of every group. Finally, the visionary leader is obligated to guide the group in the development of an overall organizational vision that either closely resembles or is complementary to that vision which he/she has already formulated. Yet, too often the area that gets a leader in trouble and delays the success of a group, is the inability to establish necessary group parameters or to develop an effective charge to the group.

A leader should develop, with the assistance of group members, a few ground rules that facilitate group development and task completion. These rules can be represented by such concepts as attendance, promptness, participation, agendas, group behavior, and even group breaks. Once established, these should be clearly explained to all group members. These explicit norms will coexist with other explicit and implicit norms that the well functioning group also establishes. The following are examples of group norms that can be useful:

1. People should be listened to and recognized.
2. It is safe to say what you think in the group. Honesty is valued.
3. Feelings are important. Group member ideas may be criticized but not group members.
4. Feelings, behaviors, and concerns of everyone in the group can be freely acknowledged and discussed.
5. Objectivity is encouraged and supported by all group members.
6. The group learns from doing things, deciding on issues, and analyzing ideas.
7. The development of an organizational vision is a unified effort and all ideas are important.

A visionary leader is well prepared for each group meeting. If he/she is not, this sends a strong message to group members that the task of vision development is not really an important one and that the whole process is a bit of a sham. The use of a premeeting checklist by the leader can facilitate success of the group as it begins its task of developing an overall vision. Some of the things that a leader can do to prepare for a group meeting are to:

1. Have fixed in his/her mind what specifically needs to be accomplished at each meeting.
2. Have reminded all group members of the time, place, and purpose of the meeting as well as what members need to bring with them to the meeting.

3. Have the meeting room reserved and appropriately arranged for the meeting.
4. Have prepared and distributed an agenda.
5. Have prepared the opening comments as well as the group charge.
6. Have developed a repertoire of ways and means to initiate participation, stimulate thinking, and create interest and support for vision development.
7. Have carefully planned and provided adequate time for the task.
8. Have gathered any data that may be needed by the group as it begins working through the vision process.

In addition to being thoroughly prepared for each meeting, the visionary leader must be able to clearly articulate to the group and each group member the nature of the group task. Too often groups are established without an appropriate group charge and the group either creates its own or disintegrates as it attempts to do so. Additionally, group fragmentation can result when the group task has not been well formulated. The result of failing to provide clear organizational parameters for the group or an appropriate group charge or task is an intense disillusionment to group members as they begin to perceive they are not being listened to by the organization or its leader. The group charge should specifically address what the group is to accomplish, develop, or design relating to an organizational vision. Given the method described in the next chapter concerning the development of an organizational vision, an appropriate group charge would be:

> Each group member will follow the process of vision development, first on an individual basis and then as a group, to develop a vision for the school or organization that best represents an ideal school or organization. Group members should not initially be concerned about implementation or actualization of the vision. Each group member should be prepared to express his/her personal beliefs and values relating to the creation of the best school possible. One should also be prepared to share ideas and compromise when necessary.

This charge establishes expectations for the group and limits the group to a certain, specific task.

The group charge is designed so that no misunderstandings of purpose or task can later arise. It is best to reiterate the charge at each subsequent meeting so that every group member remains focused on the same task. Even when the group charge is clearly stated, some members may still have difficulty in understanding or accepting the parameters and guidelines set by the charge. This is when the visionary leader's skills and knowledge of group processes and group roles becomes important. Clarity of purpose by the group guarantees success. Without an appropriate charge most groups eventually fail.

GROUP ROLES

Each group has its own personality and typically develops along the lines of one of the group theories previously discussed. Within each group, individuals often elect to take a certain role. These roles may directly relate to the task or to the individual personalities and needs of each group member. It is important that the visionary leader recognize the types of roles that may exist in a group. It is also important that a leader facilitate and support those roles which lend themselves to group productivity as the vision is developed. Conversely, the visionary leader needs to recognize those roles which may hinder the group. The leader should develop a set of strategies that may lessen the impact on the group of negative roles.

The following represent those roles which should be supported by the leader. These roles facilitate group interaction and ultimately increase group productivity. They are:

1. The Energizer: Provides energy, motivation, and drive to the group.
2. The Procedural Expert: Understands how the organization functions and understands its rules and regulations.
3. The Evaluator: Is able to dispassionately view group ideas and logically utilize them without negatively impacting group members.
4. The Opinion Seeker: Carefully seeks ideas and encourages the participation of all group members.
5. The Initiator: Suggests new or different ideas for discussion and approaches to problems.
6. The Opinion Giver: States pertinent beliefs about discussion and others' suggestions.
7. The Elaborator: Builds on suggestions of others.
8. The Clarifier: Gives relevant examples; offers rationale; probes for meaning; restates problems.
9. The Tester: Raises questions to "test out" whether group is ready to come to a decision.
10. The Summarizer: Reviews discussion, pulls it together.

11. The Tension Reliever: Uses humor or calls for breaks at appropriate times to draw off negative feelings.
12. The Compromiser: Willing to yield when necessary for progress.
13. The Harmonizer: Mediates differences; reconciles points of view.
14. The Encourager: Praises and supports others; friendly; encouraging.
15. The Gate-Keeper: Keeps communications open; encourages participation.

In addition to the above roles which are to be supported and nurtured by the leader, members occasionally choose roles which hinder a group. These negative roles can be detrimental to group productivity. It is therefore vital that the leader recognize negative roles and develop a system for handling those who hamper the group. Some examples of negative roles are:

1. The Sympathizer: Attempts to garner the group's sympathy by complaining, confessing, or condemning certain activities of the organization.
2. The Aggressor: Criticizes and deflates others; disagrees with others aggressively.
3. The Blocker: Stubbornly disagrees; rejects others' views; cites unrelated personal experiences; returns to topics already resolved.
4. The Withdrawer: Won't participate; "wool gatherer"; converses privately; self-appointed note-taker.
5. The Recognition Seeker: Boasts; excessive talking; conscious of his/her status.
6. The Topic Jumper: Keeps changing the subject.
7. The Dominator: Tries to assert authority, manipulate group.
8. The Special-Interest Pleader: Uses group's time to plead his/her own case.
9. The Playboy/girl: Wastes group's time showing off; story teller; nonchalant; cynical.
10. The Self-Confessor: Talks irrelevantly about his/her own feelings.
11. The Devil's Advocate: More devil than advocate.

The above roles only represent a portion of those which may develop in a group. Group members may change roles and could project a more positive image at one time and a more negative one at a different time. The goal of a visionary leader is to understand that various roles may be exhibited in the group. It remains incumbent on the leader to maintain focus on the group charge while nurturing those roles which assist the group to become productive. Understanding group roles allows the visionary leader to successfully work with all group members in the development of an organizational vision.

KEEPING THE GROUP ON TASK

A visionary leader is able to maintain the focus of the group on the task at hand. That essentially means keeping the group's attention and energies concentrated on the creation of an overall organizational vision. This ability to maintain focus on the task is just as important when the group subsequently establishes strategies by which the vision will be communicated and actualized.

There are several methods which can be utilized by the leader in supporting the group's actions. The first, and foremost, method is to be prepared for each group meeting. A second strategy is to employ a series of questions that will keep a group on task. An example of the type of questions that may be utilized are listed below. These questions can be used directly in conjunction with one's knowledge of group roles. The questions are:

1. Leading Questions: Useful in getting opinions from the group. Examples are, "What if. . . . ?" "How about. . . . ?"
2. Factual Questions: These gather needed information. Examples are "How many students . . . ?" "Who are the. . . . ?"
3. Ambiguous Questions: These often have more than one meaning. Examples are "Could we. . . . ?" and "Would it be possible to. . . . ?"
4. Provocative/Controversial Questions. These are designed to get a reaction from the members of the group which often provides the leader insight into their values and beliefs. Examples are: "You know that. . . . ?" and "What if we did not. . . . ?"
5. Alternative Questions: These often elicit a yes or no answer which then can be followed up by "Why?" or "What?" or "How?" Examples are "Do you agree . . . ?" and "Do you think this. . . . ?"

Questions also may be asked in a variety of ways to group members. They may be "nebulous" and not asked of any one person in particular in the group. Questions may also be "front end" loaded. This type of question typically begins with a person's name and then the question is asked. These questions can be useful in refocusing an individual in a group or in putting them back on task. A problem with this type of question is that some members automatically stop listening once they hear the person's name called and realize that the question is not intended for them. Questions also may be "rear end" loaded. This type of question finds that the name of the recipient of the question is added only after the question is asked. A "rear end" loaded question is useful because it maintains the whole group's attention to the question since no one knows who is going to be called upon until the name is spoken.

A leader with a vision is often impatient and wants to implement the vision immediately. The tendency to become overly directive must be watched. It is also important to remember that if one asks questions and expects answers that the answers should be listened to by those involved. This means the leader must recognize that good communication is a two-way street. Visionary leaders tend to want to leap into each situation and answer the very questions they ask without waiting for a group member response. This should be avoided because patience at this stage will reward the vision building process as more become empowered and supportive of the vision by being actively heard. Without a commitment from the group to develop and support the organizational vision, it is unlikely that any real organizational changes or improvements will be accomplished.

HANDLING CONFLICT

All groups eventually have some type of conflict. That conflict may come early in the development of the group or it may happen when the group is highly productive. Conflict in itself is neither good nor bad. It is the potential to be destructive or constructive that is important to a leader. The visionary leader recognizes that conflict is normal and will diligently attempt to ensure that any conflict remain constructive. An effective leader realizes that organizations, groups, and individuals can grow when conflict is successfully addressed and resolved.

Constructive conflict provides possibilities and potential for a leader to bring about group growth. Constructive conflict often centers around disagreements on goals, methods to achieve goals, values, and group focus. It may result when there is an unequal distribution of information between group members or because of disagreements on how to meet human needs in the group. Constructive conflict can be resolved through open group discussions and compromise by group leaders. A leader will never mandate that constructive conflict cease. If this is done by the leader then it allows for disagreements to remain which will eventually erupt into destructive conflict.

Destructive conflict has little or no potential for improving the group, its members, or the organization. Destructive conflict can be the result of feelings by group members such as pettiness, jealousy, immaturity, uncertainty, or indefensible feelings of injustice. Symptoms include heightened tension, frustration, threats, withdrawal by group members, verbal attacks, and intense anger. Conflicts which can destroy the group's capability to effectively function must be handled swiftly by the leader and resolved so the group can continue to function.

When conflict arises a leader may respond in several ways. He/she may ignore it and hope that it will eventually extinguish itself. This rarely succeeds especially if it is destructive conflict. The second, more viable, choice is to address the conflict situation. The steps for resolving a conflict are quite simple but do require a degree of patience and tenacity on the part of the leader. First, the conflict must be openly acknowledged. It must then be examined by the group. The leader needs to be able to accurately state the nature of the conflict to the group. This is where group members also can be extremely helpful. They may possess an insight into the problem which the leader may not have. Once the nature of the conflict has been clarified, it is then necessary to determine if there are any areas of agreement between those in conflict. All points of disagreement must also be recognized at this time. The next step is to generate as many alternatives as possible to resolve the conflict and then reach an agreement as to which alternative can best be utilized to resolve the situation. The idea is to establish a win-win possibility so that there are no real losers in the conflict. A plan is developed with the chosen alternative. The leader then will summarize the plan and get a firm commitment from group members to implement the resolution strategy. The plan is implemented and the conflict hopefully resolved. The group may then move on to future challenges as it fulfills its responsibilities as established in the group charge. Resolving a conflict should not be seen as a power play by anyone but rather a means to maintain group productivity.

A visionary leader must possess the skills of listening, conceptualizing, interpreting, responding, and synthesizing in order to successfully resolve conflict. The leader must also have a sense of timing and clear communication abilities. It is important to know when to introduce structure, use authority, defer or ignore, seek consensus, and show concern. The visionary leader has the ability to be descriptive, forthright, and patient throughout the process.

One must be able to recognize some of the typical group problems that can lead to conflict. Some of these potential problems can be avoided if the group understands its task and how it is to accomplish it. The following are some of the typical group meeting problems that can generate a conflict situation. They are:

1. Multi-headed animal syndrome: Everybody going off in different directions at the same time.
2. Confusion between process and content: Are we talking about how to discuss the topic or what topic to discuss?
3. Personal attack: Attacking individuals rather than their ideas.
4. Traffic problem: Difficulty in leaping into the conversational flow and getting a chance to participate.
5. Unclear roles and responsibilities: Who is supposed to be doing what?
6. Data overload: Holding on to too many ideas in your head at one time.
7. Repetition and wheelspinning: Going over same old ideas.
8. Win/lose approaches to decision-making: Partial solutions, compromises, polarization, and low commitment.
9. Confused objectives and expectations: Why did you call the meeting and what is the group supposed to be doing? Hidden agendas.
10. Unresolved questions of power and authority: Do we have the authority to make this decision?
11. Problem avoidance: Everything is fine. There are not problems around here.
12. General negativity and lack of challenge: There is nothing we can do about it, so why try?
13. Communication problems: Not listening to or understanding what others are saying or making faulty assumptions.
14. Poor meeting environments: Can't hear, can't see, too stuffy.
15. Personality conflicts: Lack of openness and trust, underlying tension, racism, and sexism.

If conflict is not resolved, the group may eventually destroy itself. The ability to recognize whether the conflict is constructive or destructive is vital. It is just as important that a leader know how to effectively mediate a destructive situation so that the group can continue to grow and be productive. The visionary leader recognizes situations that have the potential to develop into conflicts and seeks to resolve any problem before it becomes a major issue. The visionary leader does not seek conflict nor does he/she shy away from it. Indeed, the visionary leader views conflict as inevitable but as a means by which the group can mature as it continues the process of vision development.

CONCLUSION

A visionary leader understands groups and how they develop. He/she also comprehends group roles and the inevitability of conflict. The visionary leader accepts that the group charge with well established group parameters holds the key to the development of an overall group vision. Knowledge of groups provides the visionary leader with the patience and understanding necessary to ensure the success of the group. He/she is willing to take the time to nurture a group so that it may ultimately be successful.

The visionary leader accepts that the involvement of others is the only way to guarantee the creation of a meaningful organizational vision. The development of the vision gives a new sense of meaning to members in the organization as they commit themselves to a better future. As the group members gain a feeling of empowerment and commitment, the importance of actualizing the vision becomes a driving force. The visionary leader and the group members become joint stakeholders in the vision. Together the organizational vision is developed, communicated, actualized, and sustained. An understanding of groups and group processes provides a framework allowing the visionary leader to bring the vision to fruition.

Chapter VI

DEVELOPING AN OVERALL ORGANIZATIONAL VISION

The ability to facilitate the development of an overall organizational vision is a crucial step in the vision process. The visionary leader, guided by his/her personal vision, must be able to counsel various sized groups comprised of diverse personalities in the establishment of an organizational vision. This ultimate group vision will often closely resemble the leader's personal vision. It is imperative that the overall group organizational vision be one that is not out of sync with the personal vision of the leader. This means that the leader needs to be able to guide, cajole, facilitate, and even manipulate groups as the organizational vision is developed. This will ensure that the design of the overall vision is compatible to the leader's personal one.

The word manipulate above should not offend or surprise anyone. In reality, leaders manipulate their followers many times in different situations. If the manipulation is for personal aggrandizement or promotion, then it is obviously inappropriate. But when the manipulation is for the greater good of the organization or to resolve unnecessary roadblocks, then it is acceptable. Assisting groups so that they can function in a productive manner is representative of a positive manipulation. This can be accomplished through the structuring of the group or by establishing a group charge that focuses the group's energy and effort. Truthfully, this is leadership and should not be viewed as some type of Machiavellian evil.

The visionary leader utilizes his/her personal vision as well as his/her knowledge of group processes to guide others in the development of an overall organizational vision. As the process continues, after the establishment of an overall vision, the group then designs a means by which the vision can be communicated to others. Ultimately, the group develops a plan by which the vision may be actualized.

The process of designing an overall vision is time consuming. However, the value of this process is that the organizational vision becomes owned by those involved in the process which makes the vision much more viable and achievable. The amount of time and the patience invested at this stage will pay off through support for the vision that will be generated by those involved in the process. Leaders must be cautious at this stage and not get too impatient and force the group to move too quickly in developing the organizational vision. Speed can defeat the whole process. Consensus, acceptance, and cooperativeness need to be the guiding concepts.

UTILIZING GROUPS

The visionary leader utilizes his/her knowledge of group processes to assist the several heterogeneously constructed groups to develop an organizational vision. The developmental process is similar to that followed by the individual leader in the design of his/her personal organizational vision. The obvious difference is that since more people are involved there is a greater need for direction from the leader.

The first step is to select a variegated, cross-section of individuals who are willing to work on the development of the overall organizational vision. These individuals should represent faculty, support staff, parents, retired citizens, the business community, students, and even those who do not traditionally support the organization. It is important that group members be willing to give of their time and participate fully. If any one member participates only to block progress, that person must be effectively dealt with by both the group and the group leader.

The total group which should represent a diverse cross-section of educational stakeholders should number approximately 24 to 30. If the community is a large one, the number may need to be increased proportionately. If the community is reasonably small, then the group could be reduced in number.

The group members should be addressed by the leader and provided a relevant, viable overall group charge. The method by which the group charge is developed has been previously discussed in Chapter V. The group is advised that each individual member will develop his/her own personal vision of the organization by following a few incrementally, sequentially designed questions. Once this personal, organizational vision has been developed, then several subgroups will be created consisting of three to five members. Each person will be randomly placed into one of the subgroups.

Individual members of the subgroup will do three things. They will (1) share their separate vision statements; (2) look for similarities and dissimilarities in the various vision statements; and, (3) develop a consensus vision statement that all in the subgroup can accept and support. The success of each subgroup is dependent upon open communication between group members and the ability to arrive at a common vision.

It is important that all members understand the concept of consensus building. The leader may have to instruct the group members in how to develop a consensus. It is important that consensus be reached by each subgroup, as well as any subsequent groups, so that the overall organizational vision is fully supported by all group members. Some basic guidelines for developing consensus may be useful. The following could either be taught to the group or handed out to them and discussed in the subgroups.

Consensus is often difficult to reach. Not every ranking will meet with everyone's complete approval. Try to make each ranking one with which all group members can at least partially agree. In reaching consensus:

1. Avoid arguing blindly for your own opinions. Present your position as clearly and logically as possible, but listen to other members' reactions and consider them carefully before you press your point.
2. Avoid changing your mind just to reach agreement and avoid conflict. Support only solutions with which you are able to agree to at least some degree. Yield only to positions that have objective and logically sound foundations.
3. Avoid conflict-reducing procedures such as majority voting, tossing a coin, averaging, and bargaining.
4. Seek out differences of opinion. They are natural and expected. Try to involve everyone in the decision process. Disagreements can improve the group's decision because a wide range of information and opinions improves the chances of the group to hit upon more adequate solutions.
5. Do not assume that someone must win and someone must lose when discussion reaches a stalemate. Instead, look for the next most acceptable alternative for all members.
6. Discuss underlying assumptions, listen carefully to one another, and encourage the participation of all members.

Once each subgroup has developed a consensus organizational vision, then two subgroups are joined to share their subgroup visions. Members may also desire to share their individual visions and discuss the process by which consensus was achieved. Each subgroup, and larger combined groups, will move at different speeds. The leader as facilitator should be available to assist as needed but it is important that the leader not dictate a vision to any of the groups.

Each new larger group will then develop a viable, consensus-derived organizational vision. Since the number involved, six to ten, is still relatively small everyone will participate in developing a vision statement. The positive side of having everyone continue to participate is that all members will feel that they are an integral part of the process.

After the combined subgroups develop an overall organizational vision, they will join with other combined subgroups of six to ten members. At this point, the combined groups representing a total of four subgroups may desire to select representatives to work on the vision statement. A total number of 24 to 30 may simply be too cumbersome to accomplish much. However, the decision to use a representative system should remain with all group members and not be made by the leader. The total group will review two vision statements which originally were four or six in number depending upon the number of subgroups that were created as the process began. One should think of it as a giant puzzle that fits together successfully only with the leader's guidance and assistance. The simple diagram in Figure 7 should be useful in visualizing the process.

Each subgroup, and subsequent combined groups, should be asked a series of questions that will assist them in validating the strength of their various vision statements. These questions are:

1. Do you believe in the consensus vision statement?
2. Do you support it?
3. Will you work to actualize the vision?
4. What behaviors will you choose to model that support the vision?
5. Will you fight for the vision?

The relevance of these questions is that they force the various group members to ascertain whether the consensus vision statement represents values that are important to the individuals involved in developing the statement. If a member actively supports the overall organizational vision, then he/she becomes a powerful asset in the eventual actualization process. However, if a group member does not support the vision statement, the

Figure 7. Schematic of the Vision Development Process.

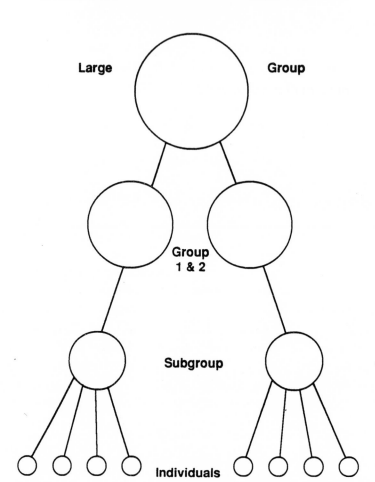

leader must step in and use his/her group skills in order to gain acceptance of the vision statement by any reticent group member. If any member who does not support the vision is not effectively addressed, then any actualization of the vision can be hindered.

The process for developing an overall organizational vision begins with each individual group member and progresses to small subgroups, then larger groups, and finally to the group as a whole. The visionary leader must carefully orchestrate the consensus building process so that the commitment by the whole group and its separate members be as strong as possible. A well thought-out group charge, carefully constructed heterogeneous groups, and a proactive leader who believes in empowerment are necessary for this portion of the vision activity to succeed.

DEVELOPING THE ORGANIZATIONAL VISION

In developing an organizational vision, individual group members must first ascertain their views of what an ideal organization should look like. This process is facilitated by the leader who initiates discussion by addressing the issues of vision development and emphasizing the importance of the vision process. It is also important that the leader provide a workable charge to those involved in the vision process. This means that all the individuals involved in developing the vision, as well as the subgroups and groups, must be clear in what they are to accomplish. The development of an appropriate charge has been discussed in a previous chapter.

Each individual group member is assisted in developing his/her personal organizational vision by the group leader. This is accomplished by first asking each person to think about the most effective school that they have seen. They are to identify any characteristics that they personally believe made the school effective. Each group member is then asked to think of the weakest, most ineffective school they have viewed. Once each individual has identified an ineffective school, they then need to determine any characteristics or attributes that made the school ineffective, poor, or weak. The intent of this activity is to begin to get each person to identify those items that make schools either effective or ineffective.

The next step is to ascertain if any of the attributes, either good or bad, apply to the school or district for which the organizational vision is being developed. Each group member identifies what they personally believe are strengths of the local school for which a vision is being developed. Conversely, they also list any weaknesses that they personally believe may exist. For instance, someone may discern that the strengths of the school are the faculty, the curriculum, and the relationship that exists between parents and teachers. The same individual may state that the weaknesses of the school relate to the age of the facilities, overcrowded classes, and an overemphasis on athletics. Obviously, the type of answers provided will often reflect the individual group member's perceptions, biases, and values. The identification of these personal perceptions are important as the process continues.

After each group member has listed strengths and weaknesses of the school, the member must then determine whether others would agree or disagree with their personal determination of the school. This allows each person to begin to understand that their personal answers often reflect their personal experiences and needs. The leader may find it useful to discuss with the total group the difference between values and beliefs, as well as how perceptions are impacted by past experiences. This may appear to slow the process, but it is important that each member feel and believe his/her involvement is important. Listening to all members, as well as asking them for direct input, assists in developing a commitment to the vision process.

Individual group members are then asked to assess other factors that may be useful in the development of an achievable organizational vision. Again, answering a series of pointed questions is useful as the process continues. Each person needs to determine if there are any "people" strengths in the school that can be capitalized upon in designing the vision. Conversely, each member needs to identify any "people" weaknesses that could hamper either the development or the actualization of an organizational vision. The recognition of strengths and weaknesses become vitally important when it becomes time to develop a strategic plan which helps the vision become a reality.

Each person is also asked to identify any external factors that could potentially be utilized in order to enable the school to function more effectively. In the same manner, individual group members are to determine if there are any external factors that could hinder either the development of the organizational vision or the actualization of the vision. Factors which may fall into either category may include items such as the community, local politics, the economy, the media, or religious groups. The failure to recognize the existence of external factors may be detrimental to the vision process and result in the development of a vision neither acceptable or achievable to the general public.

Once all of the above questions have been answered by each group member, they are ready to write their personal organizational vision statement. At this point, the leader may find it useful to re-examine the various definitions of vision that have previously been discussed. It is important that each member understand that the personal vision statement of the organization will likely reflect personal values and beliefs. It is also necessary that each member understand that their values and beliefs often are expressed in a universal or global manner but that a vision may be highly personal and that is also acceptable. The vision statements may reflect universal values such as equity or equality or personal values such as family, productivity, or love and caring. Which-ever approach is chosen by the group member is not as important as the need that the statement reflect what the individual group member really believes and supports.

Before writing the vision statement, group members should be reminded that the statement is a personal organizational vision and need not be hampered or constrained by any organizational, economic, or political realities. Instead, the focus should be on what the individual believes the school should ideally be as an organization. After clarifying this impor-tant aspect, each person should write in twenty-five words or less a vision statement which reflects what an ideal organization would be like. The written vision statement should indicate what each group member feels is the ultimate goal for the organization.

After individual group members write their personal organizational vision statements, they should test it by answering the following questions. First and foremost, does the statement really reflect one's personal values and beliefs? Secondly, does the personal organizational vision statement provide a sense of purpose which would involve others in helping achieve the vision? Does the statement represent a concept that one is willing to fight for in order to actualize it? Finally, what behavior could one personally elect to exhibit which would support the vision statement? Specifically, this means that each group member should be able to identify behaviors which they will choose to utilize which will assist in bringing the vision to fruition.

Once the above has been answered, then each group member should identify any strengths that exist or are implied in the vision statement. It is also salient to determine whether the individual organizational vision statement conflicts in any way with the values and culture of the local community. If the vision statement does conflict with local mores, each group member, and eventually the whole group, must determine how such dissonance will be responded to in a constructive manner. Essentially, this means whether the group, and really the organization, will attempt to change in some manner the local culture and its value system, or will the vision instead be compromised to adjust to local values? What will be done if the organizational vision is diametrically opposed to the values of the local community?

Although these questions may appear too philosophical, the fact is that they are critical if the vision is to be implemented and actualized. It may also seem that these questions are more important for the whole group to discuss and thus have little relevance to an individual group member. However, one needs to remember that the vision process is founded upon the belief that the whole process is only as strong as each individual's values, actions, and personal vision. It is vital that each group member have personal answers to these questions as first the subgroups and then the larger groups move through the vision development process.

After each individual group member has developed a personal organizational vision statement and tested it against the above, it then becomes necessary to share the personal statement with others in the subgroup. As personal organizational vision statements are shared throughout the several subgroups, each subgroup should ascertain any similarities and dissimilarities that may exist between the separate individual vision statements. Each subgroup should identify and list any striking differences that may exist between the various vision statements of the group members. The subgroups should also determine which areas may be similar in intent and design.

The process is really quite simple at this stage, but very time consuming. Each individual shares their personal organizational vision statement. Similarities within the statements are sought and listed. Dissimilarities are identified, listed, and discussed. The goal is for the subgroup to develop a consensus organizational vision statement that all subgroup members can accept and support. It may be useful for the group to review the consensus process as outlined earlier at this point in time. Consensus can only be achieved if each member listens carefully and responds as logically as possible, avoiding emotional appeals and diatribes against others. If one decides to change his/her view, it should not be done just to avoid an argument or to get the process over quickly. Techniques such as voting, coin tossing, or designing a point system for quick fix averaging should be avoided. Instead, the subgroup should strive for an aura of openness. Disagreements should be viewed as a way by which the subgroup may utilize diverse knowledge bases, values, and views. Individuals in each subgroup, and in subsequent activities between subgroups, should avoid developing a win-lose attitude. Everyone should be encouraged to participate, to listen, and to work together in reaching the consensus organizational vision.

The visionary leader must be extremely active at this stage of the vision building process. The leader's total actions must focus on facilitation not interference and dictation. Each subgroup or larger group has to resolve any intragroup difficulties without being told to accept a certain answer or solution. This means that the leader assists and guides but never tells a group what to do. A large proportion of the leader's skills must focus on establishing group parameters, answering questions, and subtly guiding. His/her knowledge of group dynamics and group processes will be invaluable at this point in time. Finally, the leader may not find it necessary to become involved in any type of conflict resolution. The reason is quite simple. Many people share a common value structure and belief system when it comes to education. Because of this, it is conceivable that a number of the individual organizational vision statements will be quite similar. Thus, as the subgroup begins to function at developing their organizational vision statement, the strong degree of homogeneity in the individual statements allows for a rapid, conflict free development of a vision statement which can be supported by the whole subgroup. If this type of homogeneity develops, the vision process will move very fast. However, steps of the process should not be missed or skipped. Each step must be sequentially completed so that the level of involvement and support will remain high from all quarters.

After the subgroup has developed an acceptable consensus organizational vision statement, it then joins with another subgroup and the process of sharing vision statements begins all over again. Only the subgroup consensus statements are shared. The individually developed ones need not be utilized at this stage of the process. The two subgroups follow the same process of seeking similarities and/or dissimilarities with the eventual goal of developing a consensus organizational vision statement of twenty-five words or less. At this time there may be two or three groups comprised of two subgroups each working on a vision statement.

Once these groups, consisting of six to ten persons, have developed a vision statement, it is time to combine the groups again. At this stage, the number of participants involved may simply become too many for effectiveness purposes in developing the statement. At some point in time, the groups may decide to select representatives who will proceed to the next stage where they will meet with other representatives from other groups. The representatives can be selected by the separate groups in any manner that they desire and are comfortable in utilizing. The ultimate size of the large group depends upon the number of original subgroups and the number of individuals involved in the overall developmental process. The questions utilized by subgroups and larger groups may be found in Table VIII.

Table VIII
SUMMARY OF QUESTIONS IN DEVELOPING
AN ORGANIZATIONAL VISION

What are the strengths of the school?

What are the weaknesses of the school?

What are external factors that help or hinder the proper functioning of this school?

What are various interpersonal strengths and weaknesses of this school?

How well do the various components of this organization function? And are they functioning effectively?

What does an ideal school look like?

What should the school be accomplishing?

After group members develop their individual organizational vision statements, they then design a subgroup vision statement. Subgroups then combine with other subgroups to continue to arrive at a consensus vision statement. At the end of the whole sequential process, an overall organizational vision will exist that represents a great deal of input and discussion on the part of all members of the group. That overall organizational vision represents a goal towards which those within the school and the local community are willing to actively work.

It is imperative that the overall organizational vision statement be tested against the same questions as previously used in judging the separate vision statements. These questions focus on the validity of the overall vision statement and assist in determining the degree of commitment of various stakeholders to the vision. The important questions that must be answered are:

1. Does the organizational vision statement represent values that everyone can accept, support, model, and eventually sell to others?
2. Does the vision statement accurately reflect values found in the local school and its community?
3. Does the organizational vision provide a rationale for others to become involved in both supporting the vision and ensuring that it will become actualized?
4. Does the vision provide an opportunity for people to choose behaviors that will support the vision?

If the answers to the above questions are affirmative and positive, then an organizational vision has been developed that provides the organization a viable and ultimate goal.

The role of the leader is crucial throughout this process. A worse case scenario could result in the development of an organizational vision that directly opposes the personal vision of the leader. This will not happen if the visionary leader has utilized good group processes; has provided a viable, realistic group charge; and, has actively facilitated in the development of an overall organizational vision. If the leader has effectively done his/her job, then the organizational vision will be closely allied with, and highly compatible to, the leader's personal vision. This compatibility is necessary if the vision is to be successfully communicated and actualized.

CONCLUSION

The development of an overall organizational vision is a crucial step in the total vision process. It provides an opportunity for involving others and empowering them so that the level of commitment by a variety of educational stakeholders is high enough to ensure a degree of success in actualizing the vision. The role of the visionary leader is one of counselor, facilitator, and adviser. The leader must carefully guide the members of the various groups throughout the development of the organizational vision. The leader's knowledge of group processes and group dynamics is important, but just as important is the ability to focus the group's activities so that the process does not become fragmented or trivialized because of personal agendas.

Once the organizational vision has been developed and accepted by those involved in the process, it becomes time to communicate the vision to others. It also becomes time to plan to turn the vision into a reality. The communication and actualization of the vision provides the group a further opportunity to work together to create a new organization that meets new goals as it becomes more effective.

The leader's role is not over once the organizational vision has been developed. He/she must now shepherd the group's actions with continued productivity. The vision as now developed provides an opportunity for those who were involved in the developmental process to become proactive advocates of the vision. The journey now has a destination. The leader must now move people forward so that the destination becomes a reality. Communicating the vision and planning will provide the beginning of the actualization process.

CHAPTER VII

COMMUNICATING AND ACTUALIZING THE VISION

The creation of an overall organizational vision is an essential part of the total vision process. The involvement of a diverse variety of individuals in the activity creates a core of committed people who believe in the ultimate goal of the organization as represented by the vision statement. If the charge provided to the group was effectively designed and coherently delivered, then the overall vision that has been developed should be closely allied with that of the organizational leader. A high degree of compatibility between the leader's personal vision and the group's overall organizational vision ensures an investment of time and energy by those within the organization in the next step of the process.

However, developing an organizational vision without being able to rationally communicate it to others or begin to bring it to a reality means that the whole vision building process and the resultant vision statement serves little purpose. The ability to communicate the vision is important because it signals to others, within and outside the organization, that the vision is something which is valued and achievable. The development of a sequential, coherent plan to actualize the vision indicates that the organization seriously plans to pursue the vision and that it is not just an unachievable dream.

The organizational leader's role throughout this stage of the vision process is crucial. The leader, especially during the planning process, must guide, facilitate, and assist in the creation of a rational, logical strategic plan. He/she serves as the official purveyor of organizational data that may not be accessible to everyone involved in the organization. The capacity to empower, trust, and communicate become essential tools of the leader during the planning/actualizing process.

COMMUNICATING THE VISION

Communication of the vision is vital to its success. As Rutherford (1985) determined, others have to know what the vision is and be able to articulate and publicize it in their own way. This means that the vision should be actually communicated to everyone who will listen. People need to hear it, understand it, and accept it before they can fully support it. The only true roadblock to the scope and variety of communication utilized is the limit of the leader's and group's imaginations.

The process for communicating the overall organizational vision essentially utilizes the same formula as used during the development of the vision statement. Individual members of the group will initially complete the procedures outlined below and then do so again in the subgroups and eventually the overall large group. Consensus building, sharing ideas, listening, and seeking common frameworks for communicating the vision are again the obligations of each within the group.

It is useful for the organizational leader to do two things to help this part of the process. First, he/she should review the various responsibilities of the group leader which include, but are not limited to, guiding, facilitating, and managing behavior and group focus. Secondly, the leader needs to clearly explain to the group members the means by which a vision is typically communicated as well as provide a charge to the group for developing a vision communication strategy.

A vision can be communicated in a variety of ways. Manasse (1985) referred to the development of something which represents what the organization will be like once the vision is achieved. She called this a future vision because it symbolized a better future for the organization. The focus of this communication strategy is thus "on accomplishing the possible rather than maintaining what exists" (Manasse, 1985, p. 158).

Metaphorical statements, symbols, and models are tools which assist in communicating the vision. Pronouncements such as "Striving for Excellence," "Excellence and Equity," and "A Time for Greatness" provide both impetus and direction for the organization. It must be stated that many organizations spend a great deal of time and energy in developing similar slogans and then place these slogans on everything from stationary to ink pens. The problem with this approach is that often these statements represent a public relations concept instead of a shared vision and values that have been mutually agreed upon by those involved in the organization. Communicating the vision is not an end unto itself.

Indeed, communicating the organization's vision requires each group member to utilize his/her creativity and imagination to the fullest. When communicating the vision, one should paint a picture of the ideal organization. This picture represents the optimum target for the organization. This optimum target should clearly communicate the organizational vision.

If those within the group experience difficulty in determining strategies for communicating the vision, they should read or listen to Dr. Martin Luther King, Jr.'s "I Have a Dream" speech which he presented in Washington, D.C. in 1963 before 200,000 people. This speech is full of metaphorical statements and symbols which represent Dr. King's vision of a future America. The excerpt below clearly communicates his vision:

> I say to you today, my friends, that in spite of the difficulties and frustrations of the moment I still have a dream. It is a dream deeply rooted in the American dream.
>
> I have a dream that one day this nation will rise up and live out the true meaning of its creed: "We hold these truths to be self-evident; that all men are created equal."
>
> I have a dream that one day on the red hills of Georgia the sons of former slaves and the sons of former slaveowners will be able to sit down together at the table of brotherhood.
>
> I have a dream that one day even the state of Mississippi, a desert state sweltering with the heat of injustice and oppression, will be transformed into an oasis of freedom and justice.
>
> I have a dream that my four little children will one day live in a nation where they will not be judged by the color of their skin but by the content of their character.
>
> I have a dream today.
>
> I have a dream that one day the state of Alabama, whose governor's lips are presently dripping with the words of interposition and nullification, will be transformed into a situation where little black boys and black girls will be able to join hands with little white boys and white girls and walk together as sisters and brothers.
>
> I have a dream today.

(King, 1963)

The procedure for this part of the process is essentially the same as utilized in vision development. Each individual should be asked to design a model or symbol or develop a metaphorical statement which best represents the overall organizational vision statement. One does not have to be an artist in order to design a symbol or model. What is important is that the product should clearly reflect the intent of the organizational vision to any who were not involved in the vision building process. Remember that the communication strategy selected is the primary means by which the vision will be communicated and disseminated to others.

Each person will share his/her communication concepts with others in their subgroup of three to five. The various subgroups will use the consensus building process and attempt to arrive at one model, symbol, and metaphor that best represent the unified ideas of the subgroup. As in earlier group efforts, each individual subgroup and the larger combined groups will move at different speeds. Again, as necessary, the leader should be willing to step in and facilitate group performance if the group becomes dysfunctional.

Subgroups with their models, symbols, and metaphorical statements are joined together to form a larger group of six to ten. This larger group will then arrive at a "new" consensus approach of communicating the vision. In fact, it is not uncommon for one model or symbol or statement to stand out above all the other examples advanced by group members. The consensus decision is relatively easy in this case. Occasionally, pieces of models or symbols are combined so that the most positive elements of each group's design becomes a part of the whole.

The combining process to larger and larger groups continues until the total group is ready to determine the best mechanism by which the vision can be communicated. The decision of whether this total group should be representative or consist of all members rests with the various subgroups. The total group in their discussion may elect to keep two or three good ideas or concepts which clearly communicate the vision. There is nothing wrong with this since there will often be opportunities to communicate the vision in several different ways at various times. The idea is to create a group that buys into the chosen manner of communicating the overall organizational vision. Group and individual commitment is vital to successfully communicating the vision.

As part of that communication commitment, each group member should be asked to determine how they as individuals will effectively communicate the vision to others within and outside the organization. The active communication of the vision cannot reside in the control of an amorphous "they" but instead must rest with each member of the group who devised the vision and determined the manner by which it would be communicated. Whether the individual be a board member, administrator, teacher, student, or community leader, each has an opportunity to uniquely contribute to the communication and actualization of the vision by his/her actions.

The commitment to communicate vision by one's individual activities is extremely powerful because it calls for a constant and consistent involvement in modeling the vision. It also serves as a type of verbal contact whereby one's level of engagement in the vision process can be monitored by those who have agreed to the vision undertaking.

ACTUALIZING THE VISION

The concept of actualizing the vision, or bringing it to reality, refers to both short- and long-term planning. One may decide to use one of the many commercial programs that describes strategic planning, but it is important to remember that the involvement of those in the vision process to this point in time should continue into planning and goal setting. Perhaps one of the best places to begin the actualizing process is again with the group that has developed the overall organizational vision statement and has designed a mechanism by which it may be communicated.

If it is decided to utilize one of the many strategic planning programs that exist, then it is imperative that the program has certain features or components. These features and components include:

1. An analysis of stakeholders;
2. The use of demographics;
3. A complete competition analysis and threat analysis;
4. An indepth SWOP approach (strengths, weaknesses, opportunities, and problems);
5. A review of past performances;
6. Operational plans and goals with alternative strategies;
7. Planning assumptions;
8. Implementation procedures;
9. An evaluation cycle; and,
10. An opportunity to reformulate/reconceptualize the strategic plan.

Although much of the true planning should be done by experts or those trained in such matters, the vision group should be able to assist, especially in the goal setting aspects.

The groups, individually and as a whole, have identified and discussed the strengths and weaknesses of the organization. For them, this is a good place to begin setting goals. By again utilizing the consensus process, have the various subgroups identify short-term goals, one or two years in duration, which build on the organization's strengths, while recognizing its weaknesses, and which assist in bringing the organizational vision to fruition. The caveat from earlier chapters should be remembered at this stage: Visionary leaders and thinkers refuse to allow political, economic, or social realities to stop the attainment of established goals. Just because the organization has never accomplished something such as the vision, doesn't mean it cannot do so. Both the leader and the group members should remind themselves that negative behavior leads to negative production. The key is to determine ways around any systematic blocks while continuing to focus on the vision.

The consensus process should allow the group to determine five to eight short-term goals. These goals may not all be achievable, but it is important to include several which can be reached. At the same time the short-term goals are established, group members should also identify long-term ones. Long-term goals may represent a future as far away as six to ten years. After goals have been established, a plan must be devised which will achieve the goals. It is important that the goals, both short- and long-term, directly reflect the vision. It is just as relevant to remember that the best goals are those which allow some flexibility. Thus, it is quite possible that a short-term goal could become long-term and a long-term goal may become short-term. The key is to continue the movement of the organization toward the vision. By accepting that goals are flexible, one recognizes that the organization is often impacted by external societal forces which may change the nature of the organization's clients and needs.

Establishing short- and long-term goals as targets provides those within the organization something to strive toward. Earlier, in the listing of components of a strategic plan, a threat analysis was identified as a necessary aspect. Threat analyses serve several purposes. They essentially allow for the determination of any internal or external events or activities that could directly or indirectly negatively impact the achievement of the organizational goals. The identification of such threats is only a portion of the analysis process. For instance, one may identify a strike or tax revolt as a threat. It then becomes important to determine if the threat is high, low, or nonexistent. Once this has been concluded, then contingency plans can be made on how the threat should be resolved.

Nothing will happen simply because goals have been established. It is important to develop steps to actualize the goals which are logical, sequential, and achievable. As the procedures for goal fulfillment are developed, it is useful to consider several elements. First, is the primary method chosen to achieve the goal one of emulation? In other words is a specific program/method being selected that has been successfully utilized in other organizations. Or, is the method chosen to effectuate the goal one which is proactive and innovative and represents a departure from the normal organizational response? The third possibility is that the method selected is simply reactive to a situation. If the response is reactive, then in all probability the establishment of the goal has been dictated by the problem and not the vision.

Certainly the cost of the method or procedure chosen to attain the goal is of importance to most organizations. Cost does not always equate to actual dollars but may also reflect the impact on those within the organization and their level of productivity. It is impossible to avoid consideration of cost when deciding on goals and whether they are short- or long-term ones.

After goals have been identified and the methods of attainment selected, a system of monitoring and evaluation needs to be established. In many organizations, those within the organization become so enamored with the planning process that an evaluation system to determine the level and degree of success is neglected. Certainly the overall vision statement serves as the ultimate means by which one may evaluate organizational success, but it is essential that points be established throughout the planning and actualizing process that evaluate and monitor goal attainment. Evaluation and monitoring provide necessary information that may be used to alter or diversify the goals.

Throughout the planning process, the group should continue to function in a collaborative manner. Goal setting and planning works best when the organizational vision serves as an umbrella for all of the organization's activities. Questions or activities which relate to outcomes, outputs, inputs, products, and processes are determined in direct relationship to the actualization of the vision. The establishment of goals and strategies for the organization provides an excellent opportunity to maintain the focus on the overall organizational vision. It also presents an occasion to communicate effectively to those within and outside the organization. If short- and long-term goals are realistic while at the same time reflective of the vision, it ensures a better use of the organization's resources since the goals are more focused on where the organization wishes to be in the future.

There are numerous concepts and permutations related to the planning process. The actual procedure selected is not as important as the inherent belief that the planning process should be vision driven. This is a departure from what normally happens. A typical strategic plan often represents tradeoffs, alternatives, costs, and situational analyses. If the vision represents the organization's ultimate goals and reflects the values of those within it, then the vision should dictate the majority of the decisions, whether they be short- or long-term.

CONCLUSION

The development of the organizational vision represents the culmination of the efforts of a group of diverse individuals and the visionary leader. However, unless efforts are made to communicate the vision to others, the vision serves little purpose. Communication of the vision may come in many forms but the only limitation to the scope and variety of communication strategies is the limit of one's imagination. The more the vision is communicated to others, the more others begin to communicate it. The communication process is a bit like a contagious reaction that inexorably moves the organization toward the vision.

Yet, communication is not enough. The visionary leader engages others in the process by actively involving them in decision making, problem solving, and goal shaping. This involvement not only further builds the collegial and collaborative atmosphere that began as the vision was developed but focuses the total organization on what is to be accomplished. The identification of what is to be accomplished is most often represented by goals. These goals are not achieved without effort on the part of the visionary leader and those within and outside the organization.

The establishment of goals to actualize the vision calls for a schema for bringing the goals to fruition. This necessitates careful planning best represented by several strategic planning possibilities and models. The planning process is as important as the vision process. The vision guides the planning, but planning poorly done can destroy the vision. Both are part of the effort to create an organization that represents an optimum future.

The visionary leader understands that communicating the vision, goal setting, and planning are but a continuation of the effort to actualize the vision. Since turning a vision into a reality may take much time and effort, it is important to maintain the focus and sustain the process. Sustaining the vision process calls for opportunities for member renewal and continued planning.

The journey continues in bringing the vision to a reality.

Chapter VIII

SUSTAINING THE VISION PROCESS

The sustainment of the momentum toward communicating the vision and actualizing it is an important component of the whole vision process. The visionary leader should carefully observe for any tendencies from those within the organization which lessens the level of intensity directed toward the attainment of the vision once the overall organizational vision statement has been developed and organizational goals have been established. This susceptibility to diminished effort is often related to the fact that some may now believe it is not "their" job to keep the vision process viable. Nothing can be further from the truth. The vision will simply not become real without a sustained, coordinated effort by those within and outside the organization.

If there has been a prolonged, industrious attempt by the visionary leader to engage others in the vision development process by fully utilizing shared decision making and problem-solving strategies in determining the organizational vision, then there will be a strong level of commitment to the vision from those who were involved in any shared organizational activities used to shape the vision. The proactive involvement of others in the vision building steps described in earlier chapters not only produces a sense of organizational collegiality but exhibits to all that which has been collectively determined as organizationally important (Peterson, 1986).

Sustaining the vision process represents an effort to empower those who share the commitment to the organizational vision by allowing them to communicate the vision concepts to others while they actively pursue organizational goals they helped establish. The organization must also exhibit support for the vision by institutionalizing the vision into routine daily organizational activities. Sustenance of the vision process comes from those who were part of the development process as well as the leader or administrator. Both entities must make every effort to sustain the process and maintain organizational focus.

103

SUSTAINING: THE ROLE OF THE GROUP MEMBERS

The individual members of the large group who were involved in the creation of the overall organizational vision become a vital element in sustaining the vision process. Group members have numerous opportunities throughout the typical work day to communicate the vision and model behavior that supports it. The appropriate use of such possibilities assists in maintaining a commitment to the vision by organizational members. In fact, the degree of interaction related to the vision among organizational staff members and between staff and the general public often dictates not only the degree of support for the vision effort but also whether it succeeds or fails.

Individual group members should consciously seek to model behaviors which support the vision. There should be regularly scheduled opportunities for the original group to reassemble and discuss how each person has modeled the vision daily through his/her behavior and daily activities. Individual members may desire to maintain a log of activities for sharing with other group members. It is important to note that people should not be forced or coerced into exhibiting certain behaviors, but it is relevant to impress upon everyone that the actualization of the vision is deemed to be an important and serious aspect of organizational life. The sharing of activities, behaviors, and individual demeanors, by whatever method selected, provides a level of assistance and support for those within the organization who may have difficulty in grasping the importance of the vision or in choosing behaviors which contribute to the attainment of the vision.

The concept of "practice what you preach" is also useful in determining how well the vision is being communicated to the general public. Modeling of behaviors and utilizing various activities are only two of many ways that group members will discover which communicate the vision effectively. Members often discover unique ways to communicate the vision to others. It must be remembered that these strategies would be additions to the methods agreed upon earlier by the group, as described in Chapter VII.

An important way by which group members can sustain the vision process is to utilize vision language in their daily, work-related activities. Vision language represents the concepts established during strategic planning or by any goal-setting process. The language should represent not only what the organizational vision is but reflect how the vision becomes a reality. Emphasis on goals, an orientation towards the future, a common belief in improvement, and an understanding of the total vision process represent separate components of a collective vision language. If such a common language does not exist it can indicate that organizational members do not understand the vision or are not actively involved in actualizing the vision or sustaining the process.

One way to determine the existence of a vision language is to ascertain whether those who were in the original group which designed the vision communicate its concepts differently from those who were not part of the vision building process. If the language spoken relating to organizational goals, plans, and an organizational future is different within the two groups then the assumption can be made that a vision language does not exist across all strata of the organization. Indeed, it may be that only the group which developed the organization vision understand and speak the vision language. If this is the case, then either the vision has not been well communicated throughout the organization or a vision elite has been created among those "in the know" who were involved in developing the organizational vision. Neither result is acceptable and will hamper actualizing the vision and sustaining the vision process. This is why communicating the vision is so important.

Finally, members of the original vision building group, as well as others, need to evaluate themselves and the organization periodically as the vision is pursued. This intermittent evaluation is a check to determine whether or not the organization and its members are still on the course established as part of the planning process seeking to actualize the vision. The evaluation is in actuality a test of organizational focus and commitment to the vision. This periodic check of the organization allows for any necessary adjustment pertaining to organizational goals. It also provides an opportunity to assist any person in need of guidance.

The roles chosen by the original group members and others are important because their various daily activities, discussions, behaviors, and practices keep the attention on the vision and its actualization. Without an effort to sustain the vision process, the organizational sense of direction can become muddied and eventually lost.

SUSTAINING: THE ROLE OF THE VISIONARY LEADER

The organizational leader must actively work at sustaining the vision process. The AASA monograph, *Challenges for School Leaders* (1988), identified two important components that not only facilitate the imple-mentation of the vision but also assist in sustaining the process. The first aspect described was to periodically free leaders from administrative tasks so that a type of renewal could take place for them as they are allowed to attend meaningful workshops, conferences, or visit other organizations which have been identified as effective. These organiza-tions visited should also possess a strong vision of the future. The second suggestion was to provide an opportunity for the administrative staff to spend quality time in evaluating organizational strategic plans and to further plan to actualize the vision as necessary. The release time from administrative duties could also be used to reestablish and reinforce short- and long-term goals for the organization. This two-prong approach supports the belief that the visionary leader and others in leadership roles must be provided ample opportunities to renew themselves and expand their expertise as well as time to evaluate programmatic approaches to vision achievement.

The two approaches suggested above should not imply that they represent the only way the visionary leader can sustain the vision process. In fact, daily activities of the leader provide better opportunities by which the vision process may be sustained and strengthened. A leader most often communicates the importance of the vision through his/her behavior, words, and nonverbal actions. If the organizational vision is important, and if the goal is to bring the vision to fruition, then the leader must understand and accept the need to appropriately model the vision as well as use vision oriented language.

The leader should also maintain the organizational focus on the vision by continuing to facilitate communication regarding the vision and support the means to attain it with the staff. This implies that time will be set aside to allow discussion of the vision and how to bring it to a reality. This does not mean debating the vision. Instead, the discussion should focus on developing a common vision language, support of long- and short-term goals, and efforts to determine that everyone within the organization understands and accepts the importance of the vision. A leader's efforts to sustain the vision should address not only his/her personal endeavors but also others within the organizational structure.

A true visionary leader will take every opportunity to reemphasize the vision. This continual affirmation of the vision can be supported through the allocation of funding or materials which assist in actualizing the vision. The leader should also systematically and judiciously utilize management strategies, instructional opportunities, expedient scheduling possibilities, and reward and recognition structures to maintain the organizational focus. Visionary leaders sustain the vision process by initiating, monitoring, facilitating, and orchestrating events in order to actualize the vision. The truly effective visionary leader constantly strives to create an organizational climate that enhances productivity and achievement.

In order to determine an acceptable level of productivity and achievement within the organization, it is necessary that some system of internal standards be mutually agreed upon and consistently used. Although a portion of these internal standards may be represented by the identification of short- and long-term goals, others may need to be established. It is beneficial to identify specific standards of behavior and productivity which significantly assist in the actualization of the vision. Within a school, those standards could reflect teaching, instructional goals, student behavior, and expected curricular outcomes. Any additionally identified internal standards should represent the effort of all to meet organizational goals as well as a means to support the vision effort.

The visionary leader must consistently model, communicate, and evaluate organizational efforts in order to sustain the vision process. The visionary leader must maintain his/her personal efforts to actualize the vision while assisting others to continue their attempts to do so. Sustaining the vision represents a continual focus on the organizational vision by the leader and others within the organization.

CONCLUSION

Successfully sustaining the vision process represents a combined effort of both the visionary leader, the individual group members who developed the vision, and others in the organization. Without this united effort, and the focus on the vision which it brings, the whole vision process becomes one which, at best, represents only a dream and, at worse, a nightmare that frustrates everyone.

However, by establishing measurable goals and internal standards, the vision process becomes a means by which the total organization can be improved. Continually focusing on the vision provides the organization a sense of direction and purpose. If the leader fails to model supportive behaviors or fails to utilize vision-oriented language, then many within the organization will neither understand the importance of the vision nor support its actualization. If group members do not actively support the vision, other organizational members will not deem it essential and will not support the vision process. A sharing of appropriate vision-oriented activities and behaviors suggests to everyone that the development of the organizational vision was not just an unimportant organizational activity but, in fact, represented the primary mission of the organization.

Sustaining the vision process necessitates a constant focus on the preferred organizational future. It also means a periodic evaluation and underscoring of vision goals. Additionally, the sustainment of the vision connotes an opportunity for the renewal of human energy and a suitable utilization of resources so that the organizational focus on the attainment of the vision remains strong. With everyone consistently and constantly working together, the vision effort can be effectively sustained.

Chapter IX

CONCLUSION AND FINAL COMMENTS

The educational system of this country has been criticized and heartily condemned by various groups and organizations for the past ten years. The publication of *A Nation at Risk* (1983) proved to be a catalyst for a myriad of other reports and recommendations. The federal government, as well as every state legislature, believed that the educational institution was in trouble and rapidly responded with new laws and mandates that were designed to "fix" the system. Educators were characterized as reactionary and protective of old ways that would no longer suffice. The educational systems of Japan and Germany were viewed as the best in the world and any educator who questioned this assumption was publicly castigated.

This constant and unrelenting assault upon the educational system caused teachers and administrators to withdraw from the educational debate and forced them into an operational mode best described as acquiescent and passive. The result of their withdrawal from an enlightened educational debate was that politicians and educational dilettantes developed policies of far ranging impact. Many of these policies were founded in illogical educational theory or practice.

The reform barrage came in waves. The first focused on top down mandates and directives from state legislatures. Sadly, many areas have yet to escape from this first wave which was perhaps the most far reaching and demanding of the waves of reform. A second wave brought concepts for which administrators and teachers were ill prepared. Although this second surge, with a focus on teachers and their involvement in daily operations, was more welcome than the first, it has experienced limited success. Many would like to point an accusing finger at administrators for the failure of site-based management and teacher empowerment in some schools. Yet, the truth is that the fault must be more broadly shared. Teachers were ill-prepared, and even unwilling in some instances, to be empowered or make operational decisions. The second wave of reform resulted in a high degree of organizational disequilibrium in some settings. The effect was that no one felt fully comfortable with the changes because they were still trying to meet the mandates imposed from the first reform wave. The third wave most recently began. This wave clearly addresses students and their needs. Yet the third wave, if it really does exist, remains murky and unfocused because of its inseparable ties to the first two waves.

Two things are abundantly clear from this current reform movement. The first is that this reform is inexorably different from any previous reform movement in the history of American education. It has lasted longer and has had a greater impact than previous movements, albeit not always beneficial. The second is that the reform movement is doomed to eventual failure without the support of school administrators. If reform is to succeed, school administrators must become proactive leaders who possess a vision of what their schools should become.

When one reviews the dozens of reform reports with their recommendations, one cannot help but be struck by the fact that the reports often reflect the political agenda of the group who either sponsored or wrote the report. Thus, it should be no surprise to the reader that the National Endowment for the Humanities recommended more humanities in schools or that the National Science Foundation called for increased science requirements. This "report for report's sake" often led to policy makers and politicians responding in a like manner. And so it was that in many ways "reform for reform's sake" became the reality. The result was that the reform agenda often reflected the need for some type of change without establishing a clear organizational destination. Additionally, much of the reform effort often failed to recognize or understand the sheer organizational complexity of the local school. Schools and their communities, all 16,000 districts in this country, are uniquely different. So it becomes evident that without a clear focus on what the local school should be, there can be no vision, no future orientation, and no ultimate destination.

The need for an educational vision is understandable when one looks at the result of the last few years of reform. Are schools better today than in 1985? Are test scores better? Are learning outcomes well established? Are teachers and administrators working together in a more positive, cooperative manner? Are citizens happier with the American educational system? Has the United States closed the productivity gap between this country and Japan or Germany? And finally, do we, as either a nation or local school district, have any idea where education is heading?

The answer is too often more in the negative than in the affirmative. Certainly, there are some schools where good things are happening and where there is a tremendous sense of direction. But, there are too many schools where educators wait for the next onslaught of reform while going through half-hearted attempts to address early reform efforts. What is the difference between the highly productive schools and those who are not educating all children?

The schools which have been successful, and which have a sense of direction, possess a vision of the future. It may not be specifically called that, but clearly someone, most probably an administrator, has a vision, a picture of the school at its optimum. How does one get a vision? Is one born with it? Is there a magic formula or elixir that administrators and teachers could use? The answer is not as simple as it may appear.

A vision most often is initially espoused by the school's leader. This personal vision reflects his/her personal values and life experiences. The vision becomes the force which drives a leader. He/she believes that anything is possible and refuses to allow political or economic restraints to derail the vision. This does not mean that the visionary leader is not a realist. What it does say, is that a visionary leader accepts reality and recognizes its constraints while continuing to seek avenues that will bring the vision to a reality. The process of vision actualization is not a straight line but more often one convoluted with detours and roadblocks which must be vanquished.

One thing the visionary leader knows for sure is that the journey to actualize the vision cannot be made alone. The leader involves others in developing an overall organizational vision, a way to communicate that vision, and the plan by which it is actualized. This involvement of others requires the leader to understand group processes, human behavior, roles, leadership styles, and human needs. It also requires that he/she be able to guide, facilitate, cajole, and manipulate outcomes so that the organizational vision with its goals is closely aligned with his/her personal vision. If the personal vision of the leader and the organizational vision are not closely correlated then there really is no possibility that the process will succeed. Without a mutual relationship between the visions, then the leader and the followers are on two separate and divergent paths.

But when the organizational vision and the personal vision are closely aligned, the goals of creating an exciting, productive organization is unstoppable. In fact the only thing that can stop the vision from being actualized is the failure to plan, to sustain the effort, and to institutional-ize the vision. A vision just doesn't begin nor does its realization. Both take hard work and dedication on the part of the leader and his/her subordinates.

This book is designed to provide one with a process by which a personal vision and an organizational vision may be developed. It supplies one with information about how to structure groups and effectively guide them through the organizational development phase. It also provides a structure for developing a communication strategy for the vision and a way to plan to actualize the vision.

The development of a vision is not for everyone. Some administrators are not capable of it because of their training or their personal beliefs. They simply prefer to be managers and avoid any leadership activities that may change the status quo. But for those who wish to create the best school possible and who desire to truly involve others in the improvement process, then this book should serve as a useful guide. The vision process is not easy. It is time consuming and labor intensive. It necessitates a focused effort by all educators and staff. The vision provides the ultimate destination, and when a visionary leader collaborates with the stakeholders of the school, the trip can be an exciting and rewarding one.

Welcome to true reform and educational improvement. Let the vision guide you. Enjoy the journey.

REFERENCES

Achilles, C. (1984). Forecast: Stormy weather ahead in educational administration. *Issues in Education.* 2(2), 127–135.

American Association of Colleges of Teacher Education. (1988). *School leadership: A preface for action.* Washington, D.C. Author.

American Association of School Administrators. (1988). *Challenges for school leaders.* Reston, VA: Author.

Bacharach, S.B. (Ed.) (1990). *Education reform: Making sense of it all.* Boston: Allyn & Bacon.

Bacharach, S.B., & Conely, S.C. (1986). Education reform: A managerial agenda. *Phi Delta Kappan,* 67(9), 641–645.

Barnard, C.I. (1983). *The functions of an executive.* Cambridge: Harvard University Press.

Barnes, L.B., & Kriger, M.P. (1986). The hidden side of organizational leadership. *Sloan Management Review,* 27(1), 15–25.

Barth, R.S. (1987). The principal and the profession of teaching. In W. Greenfield (Ed.), *Instructional leadership: Concepts, issues and controversies* (pp. 249–270). Boston: Allyn & Bacon.

Barth, R.S. (1988). Principals, teachers, and school leadership. *Phi Delta Kappan,* 69(9), 639–647.

Barth, R.S. (1990). *Improving schools from within.* San Francisco: Jossey-Bass.

Batsis, T.M. (1987, April). *Characteristics of excellent principals.* Paper presented at the annual meeting of the National Catholic Educational Association, New Orleans, LA.

Behling, H.E. & Champion, R.H. (1984). *The principal as an instructional leader.* Lutherville, MO: Instructional Improvement.

Bennis, W., & Nanus, B. (1985). *Leaders: The strategies for taking charge.* New York: Harper & Row.

Blake, R.R. & Mouton, J.S. (1964). *The managerial grid.* Houston: Gulf.

Block, P. (1987). *The empowered manager: Positive political skills at work.* San Francisco: Jossey-Bass.

Blumberg, A., & Greenfield, W. (1980). *The effective principal: Perspectives on school leadership.* Boston: Allyn & Bacon.

Boyer, E.L. (1983). *High school: A report on secondary education in America.* New York: Harper & Row.

Brookover, W.B., Beady, C., Flood, P., Schweitzer, J., & Wisenbaker, J. (1979). *School social systems and student achievement: Schools can make a difference.* New York: Praeger Publishers.

Burbach, H.J. (1987, November). School teachers-New kinds of thinking needed to lead education into new age. *The NASSP Bulletin. 71*(563), 1–7.

Burns, J.M. (1978). *Leadership.* New York: Harper & Row.

Carnegie Forum on Education and the Economy. (1986, May). *A nation prepared: Teachers for the 21st Century.* Washington, D.C.: Author.

Cohen, A.M. & Smith, R.D. (1976). *Critical incidents in growth groups: Theory and techniques.* LaJolla, CA: University Associates.

Conant, J.B. (1959). *The American high school today.* New York: McGraw-Hill.

Conger, J.A. & Kanungo, R.N. (1988). *Charismatic leadership: The elusive factor in organizational effectiveness.* San Francisco: Josey-Bass.

Cuban, L. (1990). Cycles of history: Equity versus excellence. In S.B. Bacharach (Ed.), *Education reform: Making sense of it all.* Boston: Allyn & Bacon.

Culbertson, J.A. (1983). Theory in educational administration: Echoes from critical thinkers. *Educational Researcher, 34* (10), 15–22.

Duke, D.L. (1987). *School leadership and instructional improvement.* New York: Random House.

Dwyer, D. (1986, Fall). Understanding the principal's contribution to instruction. *Peabody Journal of Education, 63*(1), 13–18.

Edmonds, R.R. (1979, October). Effective schools for the urban poor. *Educational Leadership, 37,* 15–27.

Education Commission of the States. (1983). *Action for excellence.* Denver: Author.

Fiedler, F.E. (1971). Validation and extension of the contingency model of leadership effectiveness: A review of empirical findings. *Psychological Bulletin, 76,* 128–148.

Fiedler, F.E. (1976). The leadership game: Matching the man to the situation. *Organizational Dynamics,* (4), 6–16.

Fiedler, F.E. (1967). *A theory of leadership effectiveness.* New York: McGraw-Hill.

Ford, G.A., & Lippitt, G.L. (1988). *Creating your future: A guide to personal goal setting.* San Diego: University Associates.

Foster, W.P. (1980). A demonstration and the crisis in legitimacy: A review of Habermasian thought. *Harvard Education Review, 50* (6), 496–505.

Gilmore, T.N. (1988). *Making a leadership change: How organizations and leaders can handle leadership transitions successfully.* San Francisco: Jossey-Bass.

Glines, D.E. (1987). Principals with vision needed to make schools exciting places of learning. *The NASSP Bulletin, 71,* (562), 92–99.

Goodlad, J. (1978, January). Educational leadership: Toward the third era. *Educational Leadership,* 35(4), 326.

Goodlad, J. (1983). *A study of schooling.* New York: McGraw-Hill.

Goodlad, J.I. (1984). *A place called school: Prospects for the future.* New York: McGraw-Hill.

Grady, M.L., & LeSourd, S.J. (1988, August). *Principals' attitudes toward visionary leadership.* A paper presented at the National Council of Professors of Educational Administration National Conference, Kalamazoo, MI.

Grady, M.L. & LeSourd, S.J. (1990). Principals' attitudes toward visionary leadership. *The High School Journal, 73*(2), 103–110.

Graeff, C.L. (1983). The situational leadership theory: A critical review. *Academy of Management Review, 8,* 285–296.

Greenbaum, S. & Gonzalez, B. (1987). Quality principals turn schools around. *The NASSP Bulletin, 71*(500), 104–108.

Greenfield, T.B. (1975). Theory about organizations: A new perspective and its implications for schools. In M. Hughes (Ed.), *Administering education: International challenge.* London: Athlore.

Griffiths, D.E. (1988, April). Educational administration: Reform PDQ or RIP (UCEA Occasional Paper #8312). Invited lecture, Division A AERA, New Orleans.

Guthrie, I.W. & Reed, R.J. (1986). *Educational administration and policy: Effective leadership for American education.* Englewood Cliffs, NJ: Prentice-Hall.

Hallinger, P. & Murphye, J. (1985). Assessing the instructional management behavior of principals. *Elementary School Journal, 86*(2), 217–247.

Halpin, A.W. (1959). *The leadership behavior of school superintendents.* Chicago: Midwest Administration Center, University of Chicago.

Halpin, A.W. (1960). Ways of knowing. In R.F. Campbell & J. Liphamm (Eds.), *Administrative theory in education.* New York: Harper.

Hersey, P. & Blanchard, K.H. (1988). *Management of organizational behavior: Utilizing human resources.* Englewood Cliffs, NJ. Prentice-Hall.

Hickman, C.R. & Silva, M. (1984). *Creating excellence: Managing corporate culture, strategy, and change in the new age.* New York: New American Library.

Holmes Group. (1986, April). *Tomorrow's teachers.* East Lansing, MI: Author.

House, R.J. & Mitchell, T.R. (1974). Path goal theory and leadership. *Journal of Contemporary Business, 3,* 81–97.

House, R.J. (1971). A path-goal theory of leadership effectiveness. *Administrative Science Quarterly, 16,* 321–338.

Johnson, C.C. (1988, August). Demographic changes: Challenges for educational administration. A paper presented at the annual meeting of the National Council of Professors of Educational Administration, Kalamazoo, Michigan.

King, Jr., M.L. (August, 1963). I have a dream. A speech presented at the Lincoln Memorial, Washington, D.C.

Kouzes, J.M. & Posner, B.Z. (1987). *The leadership challenge: How to get extraordinary things done in organizations.* San Francisco: Jossey-Bass.

Labich, K. (1988, October). The seven keys to business leadership. *Fortune, 118* (9), 58–66.

Leavitt, H.J. (1987). *Corporate pathfindings: Building vision and values into organizations.* New York: Penguin.

Leithwood, K.A., & Montgomery, D.J. (1986). *The principal profile.* Toronto, Ontario: Ontario Institute for Studies in Education.

LeSourd, S.J. & Grady, M.L. (1990). Visionary attributes in principals's description of their leadership. *The High School Journal, 73*(2), 111–117.

Lewin, K. (1947). Frontiers in group dynamics: Concept, method and reality in social science, social equilbria and social change. *Human Relations, 1*(1), 56–41.

Lipham, J.A. (1981). *Effective principal, effective school.* Reston, VA: National Association of Secondary School Principals.

Littky, D., & Fried, R. (1988, January). The challenge to make good school great. *NEA Today,* pp. 4–8.

Manasse, A.L. (1982). Effective principals: Effective at what? *Principal, 61*(4), 10–15.

Manasse, A.L. (1985). Vision and leadership: Paying attention to intention. *Peabody Journal of Education, 63*(1), 150–173.

Meares, L.B. (1988). What good leaders do. *Personnel, 65*(9), 48–52.

Morris, E. (1987). Vision and strategy: A focus for the future. *The Journal of Business Strategy, 8*(2), 51–58.

Murphy, J. (Ed.) (1990). *The educational reform movement of the 1980's: Perspectives and cases.* Berkeley: McCutchan.

Murphy, J.T. (1988). The unheroic side of leadership: Notes from the swamp. *Phi Delta Kappan, 69,*(9), 654–549.

Napier, R.W. & Gershenfeld, M.K. (1985). *Groups: Theory and experience.* Boston: Houghton Mifflin.

National Commission on Excellence in Education (1983). *A nation at risk: The imperative for educational reform.* Washington, D.C.: U.S. Department of Education.

National Commission on Excellence in Educational Administration. (1987, March). *Leaders for America's schools.* Tempe, AZ: UCEA at Arizona State.

National Policy Board for Educational Administration. (1989, May). *Improving the preparation of school administrations: An agenda for reform.* Charlottesville, VA: NPB at the University of Virginia.

National Science Board. (1983). *Educating Americans for the 21st century.* Washington, DC: Author.

Norris, C.J. & Achilles, C.M. (1988). Intuitive leadership: A new dimension for education leadership. *Planning and Changing, 19*(2), 108–117.

Office of Educational Research and Improvement, (1988, December). Youth indicators 1988 shows trends in the well-being of American youth. *Research in Brief.* Washington, D.C.: Author.

Ogle, L.T. & Alsalam, N. (Eds.) (1990). *The condition of education 1990, Vol. 1: Elementary and Secondary Education.* Washington, D.C.: U.S. Department of Education, Office of Educational Research and Improvement, National Center for Education Statistics.

Pascarella, P. (1986). Creating the future. *Industry Week, 231*(1), 68–72.

Passow, A.H. (1989). Present and future directions in school reform. In T.J. Sergiovanni & J.H. Moore (Eds.), *Schooling for tomorrow.* Boston: Allyn & Bacon.

Peters, T.J. & Waterman, Jr., R.H. (1982). *In search of excellence.* New York: Harper & Row.

Peterson, K. & Finn, C. (1985, Spring). Principals, superintendents, and the administrators art. *The Public Interest, 79,* 42–62.

Peterson, K.D. (1985). Vision and problem finding in principals' work: Values and cognition in administration. *Peabody Journal of Education, 63*(1), 87–106.

Purkey, S.C. & Smith, M.S. (1982). Synthesis of research on effective schools. *Educational Leadership, 40*(3), 64–69.

Reddin, W.J. (1970). *Managerial Effectiveness.* New York: McGraw Hill.

Roueche, J.E., & Baker, III, G.A. (1986). *Profiling excellence in America's schools.* Arlington, VA: American Association of School Administrators.

Russell, J.S., Maggarella, J.A., White, T., & Maurer, S. (1985). *Linking the behaviors and activities of secondary school principals to school effectiveness.* Eugene, OR: Center for Educational Policy and Management, Division of Educational Policy and Management, University of Oregon.

Rutherford, W.L. (1985). School principals as effective leaders. *Phi Delta Kappan, 67*(1), 31-34.

Sashkin, M. (1988). The visionary leader. In J.A. Conger & R.N. Kanungo (Eds.), *Charismatic Leadership.* San Francisco: Jossey-Bass.

Sergiovanni, T.J. (1987). *The principalship: A reflective practice perspective.* Boston: Allyn & Bacon.

Sergiovanni, T.J. & Moore, J.H. (1989) *Schooling for tomorrow: Directing reforms to issues that count.* Boston: Allyn & Bacon.

Sergiovanni, T.J. (1984, February). Leadership and excellence in school. *Educational Leadership, 41*(5), 4-13.

Shashkin, M. (1984). Participative management is an ethical imperative. *Organizational Dynamics, 12*(4), 5-22.

Shieve, L.T., & Shoenheit, M.B. (1987). Vision and the work life of educational leaders. In L.T. Hieve & M.B. Shoenheit (Eds.), *Leadership: Examining the elusive* (pp. 93-104). Washington, D.C.: Association for Supervision and Curriculum Development.

Stallings, J.A., & Mohlman, G. (1981). *School policy, leadership style, teacher change and student behavior in eight secondary schools.* Mountain View, CA: Stallings Teaching and Learning Institute.

Stedman, L.C. (1987). It's time we changed the effective schools formula. *Phi Delta Kappan, 69*(3), 215-227.

Stogdill, R.M. (1948). Personal factors associated with leadership: A survey of the literature. *Journal of Psychology, 25,*(35) 71.

Stogdill, R.M. (1974). *Handbook of leadership: A survey of theory and research.* New York: Free Press.

Sweeney, J.T. (1982). Research synthesis on effective school leadership. *Educational Leadership, 39*(5), 346-352.

Taylor, Frederick W., (1947). *Scientific Management.* New York: Harper & Row.

Tichy, N.M., & Ulrich, D.O. (1984). SMR forum: The leadership challenge—a call for the transformational leader. *Sloan Management Review, 26*(1), 51-69.

Today's numbers, tomorrow's nation. (1986, May 14). *Education Week.* p. 14.

Tuckman, B.W. & Jensen, M.A.C. (1977). Stages of small group development revisited. *Groups and organizational studies. 2*(4), 419-427.

U.S. Department of Education. (1987). *Principal selection guide.* Washington, D.C.: Author

Vroom, V.H. & Yetten, P.W., (1973). *Leadership and decision making.* Pittsburg: University of Pittsburg Press.

Wagner, C.G. & Fields, D.M. (1989, November-December). Future view: The 1990s and beyond. *The Futurist,* pp. 29-38.

Wayson, W.W. (1988). *Up from excellence: The impact of the excellence movement on schools.* Bloomington, IN: Phi Delta Kappa Educational Foundation.
Yukl, G.A. (1989). *Leadership in organizations.* Englewood Cliffs, NJ: Prentice-Hall.

INDEX